100

YEARS *of* NATIONAL
SPIRITUALISM

—— Jean Bassett MSNU ——

THE
SPIRITUALISTS
NATIONAL UNION

ISBN 0 947823 20 4

The Headquarters Publishing Co. Ltd.
5 Alexandria Road
London, W13 0NP

Printed and Bound in Great Britain by
Booksprint, Bristol

CONTENTS

ACKNOWLEDGEMENTS

I would give sincere and grateful thanks to Ray Taylor, Editor of the Two Worlds, to Tony Ortzen, Editor of the Psychic News and to Charles Coulston, General Secretary of the S.N.U. for allowing me free access to their records. Without their help I could not have completed this book in the time available. I also thank my husband for his patience and for putting up with many scratch meals over this past nine months, and Chloris Morgan for putting aside other work to help on the editing.

Jean Bassett

ILLUSTRATIONS
following page 85

INTRODUCTION

In April 1989 Jean Bassett told me that she was to write a book for the Spiritualist National Union Centenary, covering the first hundred years of National Spiritualism. Her problem was where to find the information. The records available at Head Office only covered committee meetings and apart from the last thirty years were not easily accessible. What were Spiritualist doing, what had happened in the country? I pointed to the book rack that held one hundred and three years of the 'Two Worlds' and told Jean she would find it all in the pages from 1890 up to 1960, when the 'Two Worlds' went monthly and stopped reporting news. Over the next few months, Jean became a regular visitor to our office. Midnight oil was burned and in January, 1990 it was finished: A Hundred Years of National Spiritualism.

Love it. Hate it. Ignore it. These are some of the emotions generated by the S.N.U. But you cannot dismiss it. The Spiritualist National Union has made its mark in Spiritualism's history. Its format has been emulated in other parts of the world. It could be said that the Union made Spiritualism respectable, but with its fair share of ups and downs. There were times when many of the Union's members thought that it would not survive. But here we are, one hundred years on and going from strength to strength.

I did learn one thing from this work. In chapter 4, 1905, at the close of the A.G.M., cards were circulated advertising a Spiritualist journal with the picture and the name of the just- elected president, John Adams. Will there be advertising cards issued at the 1990 Unions A.G.M. for a well known Spiritualist journal with a picture and caption:'President re-elected'?

Ray Taylor, B.A.
Editor, The Two Worlds.

PREFACE

It is rare in the history of humanity for a religion to grow out of the interest and desire of the people, rather than from the charismatic influence of one individual with revelation to perpetuate.

It is also rare to find any religious body which does not believe and preach that they alone have access to the 'truth' and thus access to eternal bliss. Who do not believe in attempting to bribe and/or corrupt their God through sacrifice, ritual or flattery; who do not elevate their priests above the people, or assume that their leaders will have special dispensation and a place in the hierarchy of the universe.

The Spiritualist National Union stands not alone but certainly lonely, within the ranks of that rarity. Having grown from the need of separate groups to formalise and strengthen their structure, from the need of individuals to come together with those of like mind and yet still be left with the freedom to think for themselves the Spiritualist National Union is an ongoing, democratic religious body which is government recognised with its own miinisters excercising the same rights as other non- conformist religions.. Established through the needs, desires and work of the people it belongs to the people.

Our history is as yet brief. It is only one hundred years since this successful, national organisation was established. It is easy sometimes to forget how young we really are. So much growth has taken place, such a vast amount achieved more than enough for us to recognise all too clearly how far we have yet to go. We who are sharing this centenary year of celebration can reflect on past achievements only in order to contemplate future accomplishments. These will be our responsibility and privilege.

3

Today, the S.N.U. is still the largest, although not the only organised body of Spiritualists in Britain. It is the only organisation to offer democracy and opportunity of education to its members, charitable protection and legal advice to its churches and societies, an alternative source to whom individuals can make complaint if satisfaction cannot be achieved at local level, and protection for all members through the security of rules which are common to all its affiliated bodies. This, our Union, is trustee to over four hundred churches and societies. It is the only spiritualist organisation to have a pool similar to a building society the assets of which are protected by a separate trust. This is so that the funds invested by the members are always safer, and available.

There have been thousands of books written about Spiritualism. Some biographical, some philosophical, very few historic, all written according to the feelings and experience of the individual. This wide variety of opinion and teaching makes it difficult for the onlooker or newcomer to understand the basic philosophy of Spiritualism. Thanks to National Organisation there has been some cohesion and we have a general basis on which to determine our belief. It has been difficult at times because that introduction is vital to the Spiritualist. All too often a lack of information about the true beliefs held by the church or society to which the newcomer is introduced leads to misunderstanding and/ or loss of interest. The basis of National Spiritualism has common roots in the essence of many religions but is tied to none. This is part of the philosophy taught in our churches. At the same time the true Spiritualist tries not to be dogmatic but to welcome all who seek to know. To remain as a group with a common understanding and yet to give each person the freedom to think and grow as a spirit will never be easy. But then to commit one's self as a Spiritualist is not an easy path to follow, for it involves a maturity of understanding and a relationship with God and the Universe which not everyone is ready to accept. Those who have committed themselves are usually those who do not, cannot, accept the opinions of others without reason. They will not blindly follow a leader and do not accept other people's version of the truth. The Spiritualist ex-

4

plores a situation and comes to a personal conclusion. Most Spiritualists are individualistic. Our pioneers were definitely so.

How then did they manage to come together to form a National organisation? When and how did the need arise? Why 'National'? Few existing books address themselves to this subject. None trace the growth of our Union, which is the body of our religion, and to which we have given our promise of allegiance

Where any history is given, it is so intertwined with Spiritualism generally that it is difficult to say: 'this is National Spiritualism; that is not'. Often this does not matter, but everyone likes to know their roots. In this small book a start has been made. Some detail is given, many generalities. As far as possible accuracy has been observed. I have tried to keep to a chronological order; there is nothing so annoying as having to work out why an event took place when it is out of sequence. This is not an academic book; I am not an academic. I hope you, the reader, will find it readable!

Jean Bassett

THE FIRST HUNDRED YEARS OF NATIONAL SPIRITUALISM

CHAPTER 1

IN THE BEGINNING

Spiritualism

Modern Spiritualism is said to have started at Hydesville, In New York State, on March 31 1848. But its phenomena were noted in previous decades and in other lands. Spiritualism did not start as a religion. Indeed, it was not even called Spiritualism; that title came later in the century. A hundred years previously, around 1750, Franz Mesmer a German working in Vienna and Paris took interest in an old belief that magnetised rods had healing properties. He developed a technique, using these rods and verbal persuasion which proved to be quite successful and popular. An offshoot of this was that in some people it induced trance conditions during which many different types of phenomena manifested. The varieties of phenomena, recorded well before 1848, were startling. Baron du Patet's investigations in France reveal virtually every type of phenomena known, except perhaps those involving photography or other modern appliances. Of course, phenomena has been known and recorded throughout the history of Man. But mesmerism had the effect of producing the right mental conditions for the potential psychic at a specified time.

The Scandinavian medium and philosopher, Emmanuel Swedenborg, born in 1685, also blazed a trail across many parts of Europe and his writings hold the seeds of much Spiritualist thought. As early as 1837 at Mount Lebanon in America, communications, received over a period of seven years from spirit, predicted the spreading of the phenomena all over the world. Andrew Jackson Davis was teaching and demonstrating his remarkable gifts in trance from as early as 1844. His great book, 'The Principle of Nature, His Divine Revelation and a Voice to Mankind', dictated while in trance to a scribe and often in front of an audience, was published in 1847.

On the morning of March 31st,1848, now known as Hydesville Day Andrew Jackson Davis recorded a dream. During the night he had heard a voice in his sleep, 'Brothers' he was told, '...the good work has begun- Behold, a living demonstration is born'. He was left wondering what the message meant. Later Podmore stated publicly that he was unwilling to assume that the words referred to the Hydesville rappings. Looking back, after a hundred and forty years it seems highly coincidental; unlikely that it could refer to anything but the events that took place at Hydesville later that day!

Katie and Margaret Fox are the first people on modern record to hold a form of conversation with Spirit. It is this fact, that they devised a code whereby questions could be answered,that made the phenomena taking place in their home so interesting. No, not just interesting, world-shattering! Joan of Arc heard and obeyed angelic spirit voices; Swedenborg 'walked with angels'; the patriarchs of the Bible spoke to no-one who was not of elevated status, usually thought to be 'God'. The Fox sisters communicated in conversation with an ordinary soul, who was able to answer questions about his recent life and death on earth.

Charles B. Rosna was not particularly spiritual, famous or wise. He did not have any great revelation to convey, just a grievance which he wanted people to know about. Was it coincidence that the Fox family moved into his former home in 1847? Many of the family had psychic ability and the sisters were at the age of puberty known to be an age of great psychic sensitivity. Psychic phenomena had been manifesting in Europe and America for a number of years with little comment, phenomena that was infinitely more sophisticated and exciting than the raps and taps which were heard at Hydesville. Swedenborg had already declared that men and women did not change drastically after death. He had founded his "New Church" on these statements but had attracted comparatively little public attention. On March 31st the 'Two-Way Link' between the spirit of Charles Rosna and Katie Fox erupted into a massive publicity exercise; not engineered by people but surely, in retrospect, by Spirit! An ordinary man had passed through the portals called death, retained intelligent memory of the event and sufficient human feelings to complain about the method of his passing.

Many claims of fraud have been levelled against the mediumship of the Fox Sisters. They personally confessed to fraud, although they later retracted this confession. Medical evidence was produced to show that they could have made loud clicks by manipulation of their joints. What is not always realised is that the very walls of the house shook with the power of raps levied against them; that this continued after the girls had been taken to a neighbour's house to rest. Those 'experts' ignored the fact that Rosna gave accurate information which could not be proved at that time, but was proved later when excavation of the cellar confirmed that he had indeed been buried there after being brutally murdered. The resulting publicity encouraged literally hundreds perhaps thousands of ordinary people to explore the possibility of communication. Many were successful and soon, as in Europe, various different forms of psychic phenomena were being manifested. People floated in chairs above the heads of those present. Flowers were apported. Trumpets blared out words and rocked to the beat of heavenly music. Some psychics started to work in public Papers were written and distributed The interest spread as no other common interest had spread before. Only a few at that time, connected the phenomena with eternal life but the potential was there and the psychological conditioning of the people in America was right.

Britain had, largely, ignored the phenomena of psychic manifestation. One or two mediums were working in public. Georgiana Eagle demonstrated in front of Queen Victoria at Osborne House in 1846. But even this did not at that time excite great attention although her later work and investigations did.. However, when in 1852 Mrs Hayden travelled from America to be introduced in England by Mr Stone, a mesmerist of note, much publicity was generated. Even more attention was given when she was joined in London by Miss Jay and Mrs. Roberts. Fierce arguments took place, often through the press, as to the authenticity of these ladies and the phenomena produced. Reports in many papers were derogatory and often untrue. The adage 'any publicity is good publicity' may not be true for Spiritualism in this era but at that time it worked to spread interest swiftly the length and breadth of Britain. It was not long before 'table-turning' became socially acceptable. Smart ladies served tea and then retired to 'communicate' with spirit. For them it was a social pass-time. But there were others for whom 'Spiritualism' became a way of life.

People Need To Relate To Each Other
In trying to understand the history of any organisation it is important to recognise why it came into being and what promoted the conditions necessary to success, or failure. Spiritualism spread slowly in Britain in comparison with America. The social conditions were very different. Britain did not have the same conditions of immigration and change; the movement among the different classes of society was far less extreme. The established Church here had retained a more powerful influence up to the middle part of the 19th century. It was a force to be reckoned with long after that period, but many people had become very disillusioned and were questioning the truth and value of traditional statements With the Industrial Revolution a great change had taken place. Working class people started to realise that they too had rights and could question the order of the Universe. People moved to cities to find work in the great industries. This was most noticeable in the Midlands. Many people having left the dominant influences of their local church did not choose to re-commit themselves in their new environment. Others chose to abandon the faith of their fathers in a rebellion against the dictatorial, often mean-minded, attitude of the clergy.

Darwen's theory of the 'Evolution of Man' made a tremendous impact. It questioned the very basis of the teachings of the Established Church. When Galileo Galilis proclaimed his discovery, that the earth is not the centre of the Universe, in the 17th century he was forced to recant. The church in England no longer had such power. People saw their traditions were open to question. The church stood firm and said they must have faith and believe; the people looked elsewhere. The Age of Reason dictated their response. Advances in all the sciences showed the possibility of proof. This new interest, psychic phenomena, fell into line on all counts. First, it could be seen and investigated. Second it was open to all, rich or poor, highborn or low. Because the whole concept was new, there were no hard and fast rules laid down to limit possibilities or participation by any sector of society. There was a tangible equality which could be seen to work.

Finally, phenomena was fascinating. Operating by no known laws, it linked the seen with the unseen, this earth with eternity.

Communicating In Groups

The exploration of Spiritualist phenomena became very popular. Generally, the formation of groups fell into three categories.

Those interested purely in the scientific aspect and who had the money to follow the work of a medium willing to submit to investigation came mainly from the South. There were many of these groups and some important individuals. These would hire the time of a person capable of producing phenomena and engage in a series of meetings in test conditions. A number of prominent scientists took this course. Some, like Lord Adare, Alfred Russel-Wallace, Nassau Senior declared their belief and braved the ridicule of their colleagues. Sir William Crookes (physicist) was prominent among these brave souls and created a sensation when he published the results of his investigations, in 1871-74, mainly with D.D. Home. The press had anticipated with glee his denunciation of the phenomena, and at first refused to publish his positive embrace of its authenticity. Although he, and others like him, faced enormous criticism and ridicule, their support was vital to the respectable growth of Spiritualism. It was this calibre of per-

10

son who formed the Society for Psychic Research. At first many mediums were willing to co-operate in these experiments but less and less consideration was shown for the safety and comfort of the medium and more onerous demands were made. Before long, the Spiritualist movement and the S.P.R. went their separate ways.

The second category were the groups devoted to the development of mediums. These were lucky enough to have a natural psychic in their midst. They witnessed the phenomena and supported the medium, their loyalty being rewarded by the results produced. There was a variety of phenomena, even as in America, but never in the excessive quantity that had been manifested abroad. There has never been an explanation given for this. It could be that the social conditions of unrest activated the faculty in more individuals there; it could be a question of the greater number of people and results being produced in ratio; possibly something to do with the difference in national temperament; possibly a mixture, no-one really knows! Because they were widely scattered the methods of controlling these groups were individual. The centre point was, of course, the medium and if the group disintegrated there were always others willing to offer their support to the central figure. It was unusual, in the early years, for more than one person in each group to develop their abilities simultaneously.

Those who did not have access to witnessing phenomena met to talk about it, to discuss the latest reports and published papers. They explored the possibility and implications of the phenomena. It was from this latter type of group, the last of the categories, the people were found who were to change the focus of attention from science to religion. The move away from the Established Church had been gradual and the gap left in the emotional religious needs of the people had not been fully realised. Many allowed materialism to fill that gap, but there were thousands who were ready mentally as well as emotionally to embrace a new faith.

Without access to a medium these people were forced to 'believe'. Belief is the foundation of any religious philosophy.

The Move Towards Organisation

At first there were very few mediums demonstrating in public and development was a hit and miss affair. There was quite a lot of guidance and advice given through articles, discussion and letters printed in magazines and papers. In an article in "The Spiritualist" in 1869, instructions were given on "How to form a Spirit Circle". In this, people were advised not only on the formation of a family circle, but were warned against fraudulent mediums and advised to prosecute such individuals if any charge had been made. In this article the assumption was made that most are mediumistic and that they would be able to produce phenomena if properly supported. Everyone wanted to 'try for themselves'. The 'word' of the century was 'fact' and Spiritualism at least attempted to prove the basis of their statements.

Within many groups, hitherto ordinary people suddenly found that their words carried weight and had importance. This resulted in attempts to form larger groups and societies. Those who had formed a new role in life as a 'Leader' wanted to continue in that role. This is why so many societies were formed, foundered and were formed again, often with the same people taking the dominant position. This, a normal part of human nature was, perhaps, more intense at that time. In our present era we are used to ordinary people taking a responsible position in society. At that time ability was only just really emerging as a pathway to success. The poor had been dominated down trodden and without influence or importance. We can scarcely imagine that degree of poverty; we cannot judge the desire to hold on to a position achieved.

Education, generally a vital requirement for success, usually had to be paid for. Hours spent in study kept the young adult from useful employment which could make a difference to the family income. It may surprise many to know that England at that time had a higher rate of illiteracy than America. If a man and his children were born to the lowly working class of society they had very little chance to move out of that trap. The class system, so despised in the middle of this century, was not just about "ladies and gentlemen" but about rich and poor; opportunity and privilege as opposed to servitude. The Established Church fully supported this system; indeed they were an integral part of it. Absolute obedience to one's 'betters' was demanded and enforced. They represented the power of God and eternity on earth, demanded and received subservience. It is no wonder that those with grit and intelligence rebelled. In Lancashire and Yorkshire, men and women found a new dignity, as well as an interest in Spiritualism. They embraced the American way, which was outside the orthodox religion of their childhood, right from the start. At first in the South many kept certain of their old practices and beliefs; they wanted Christianity, but they also wanted to investigate Spiritualism. There was an uneasy truce because the Established Christian Church utterly condemned the attempts at communication. They pronounced the practice as evil and dangerous and encouraged their members to disrupt Spiritual meetings, often violently. In spite of, or perhaps because of all these things the interest in Spiritualism grew. So did the need to join together into larger societies.

Groups Learn To Co-operate

Many individual groups had started to hire premises so that they could hold public meetings. Because there were so few mediums working in public and their own locally developed mediums had not yet been taken to the platform in great numbers, the need for co-operation was paramount. It was also a financial necessity. It was not cheap to pay for the travel and keep of a medium found to be willing to attend, and few had money to spare. Groups amalgamated within districts and quite a few successful organisations were formed over the years. Soon some enlightened people recognised the need for not just district but for national organisations. At first this remained just recognition. National Organisation is not easy, even now with swifter methods of travel and when more people have more time and money to spare for such travel. In the last century it took a very determined person great effort to find time and money. Holidays were much shorter, wages lower; communication by telephone was not common and postage, in modern comparison, higher. No organisation can exist without funds.

Equally, no organisation can even start without determined co-operation.

It is fairly easy to co-operate in small areas. But when people are coming from the far ends of the country they have to start working together as strangers; This is more difficult to achieve. In the Midlands successful District Societies were formed. They pooled ideas, expenses and dreams. Their committees were made up of representatives from all the little local groups. They took on the responsibility for booking mediums, distributing literature and generating interest in Spiritualism. The missionary work was a vital part of their role and was a great influence in society. In 1875 the Lancashire District Committee, representing 16-18 areas reported that nearly every town and village in their district had been visited. The system had a very loose structure and was based on voluntary co-operation. There was a small executive and about forty representatives of groups who were re- elected quarterly. Other areas tried to copy this format but could not achieve the same success, possibly because there were no formal rules or constitution. The disintegration of such District Societies was inevitable. It was not just lack of finance. Human nature was the main obstacle to continued success. Spiritualists did not yet think of themselves as part of a structure. Those who had found individual influence in their own small area did not want to be dominated by anyone who might have greater ability or charisma. Although the general trend of thought led them to consider themselves as a religious group, they could not visualise that religion as on a par with the established, conventional religions. Loyalty was given where benefit was derived and to people who were known personally and trusted. Times had been too hard for most people who converted to Spiritualism to pay the expenses of distant committees. The idea of control by voting for action had not yet been introduced on the larger scale.

CHAPTER 2

NATIONAL ORGANISATION

The concept of National Organisation started as far back as 1865 in Darlington. Only twenty-five individuals attended the meeting and they were not representative of any group or society. They did establish the Association of Progressive Spiritualists of Great Britain but this was more a title than reality. Even the Spiritualist Press didn't report this meeting, possibly because it was not Christian and this omission still offended many people. James Burns made the most of this; he branded the press 'sectarian' and prepared the start of a new journal, a non- christian organ. When this was launched in 1867 it was called "The Human Nature". James Burns was a complex character; he managed to turn most things to his advantage. He produced quite a lot of pamphlets and literature about Spiritualism. He also managed to virtually corner the market in sales of these at one time, in such a way that it appeared that his interest was mainly financial and yet he supported the movement, wanted a National body and was instrumental in starting a number of groups in the London area. No easy task, for there was a lot of violent opposition.

Generally, the press and the public were against national organisation. Many valid fears were expressed and arguments printed. Many felt that 'Individual freedom would be threatened'; 'Local groups were adequate'; that 'Those rising to power would be interested in Office rather than Spirit work;' that 'Organisation would destroy the essence of Spiritualism and the spontaneity of mediums; oligarchy would prevail and ordinary individuals would have no voice in the eventual government'. All these arguments had an element of truth in them and the fears of the people prevailed. The years passed; a second at-

15

tempt to form a National Organisation, made by J.J. Morse in Liverpool, was also doomed to failure. Local associations still flourished. Some, like the Marylebone Association would progress into this century, (albeit with changes of name). The Marylebone Association changed their name when they moved to Belgrave Square and are now known world-wide as the Spiritualist Association of Great Britain (SAGB).

Groups joined to make societies, sometimes large, sometimes quite small. They flourished for a while, then failed. Generally the larger the number involved the sooner they disintegrated. There were numerous reasons for the failures. Often the initial enthusiasm waned beneath a lack of support and the need for continuous effort. Organising meetings can be hard work, and the task usually falls on the same people time after time. The need to find suitable premises and the cash to pay for them was a real problem in many cases. Sometimes, because a group grew around the charismatic influence of one person it collapsed when that person moved on, or another strong character challenged the leader's authority. Still the need to come together overcame the disappointments of the past and further attempts were made. Many straws can cover much ground, but they are subject to the vagaries of the climate. To be strong they need to be bound together. In unity rather than in numbers lay the hope for the future development of Spiritualism. The problem was finding a system that would eradicate the very real fears of the individual while binding all the separate groups under a common cause.

National Federation

In 1887 a new Spiritualist journal was started by Emma Hardinge Britten which was to prove very important in the story of National Spiritualism. The 'Two Worlds' is still published although now on a monthly not a weekly base. It was then known as 'The People's Popular Penny Spiritualist Paper.' Emma Hardinge Britten edited this paper for five years, and more than any other editor is identified with the paper. Emma was a firm and fervent advocate of National Spiritualism. A vociferous writer on many varied subjects, she

16

had the vision to realise that Spiritualism could be more than a cult emerging from a fashionable fad, or from the work of scientists eager to explore a different form of phenomena. A cult is short-lived, where-as if a national movement emerged, organised and permanent in nature, we would be more readily recognised as a religious movement. In 1888 the 'Two Worlds' sponsored a competition. The prize-winning essay, by Phillip Seymour, outlined his proposals for National Organisation on very similar grounds to those followed by the defunct Lancashire District Association. Following on from this, Emma wrote several articles supporting the idea, and on March 21st 1890, she proposed that an inaugural meeting be held in the second week of April, inviting all who were interested in National Organisation to attend.

That meeting was counted as the first of the Federation. But it was actually just an informal gathering of people who decided to support another attempt at National Organisation. They agreed on a date and place for a conference to be held: the first Sunday in July, the 6th, in the Co-op Hall, Manchester. There sixteen members were appointed as Council. Dr and Mrs Britten, Mr and Mrs E.W. Wallis, sub-editor 'Two Worlds' Mrs Williamson, J.J. Morse, W.Johnson, J.B. Tetlow, H. Boardman, P. Lee, Mr Raynor, Mr J.Gibson, R. Fitton, T. Brown, J. Simkin and F.Tomlinson (Treasurer). Eight thousand circulars were sent out to elicit the feelings of Spiritualists about this meeting. The response was excellent: representatives from all over the country agreed to attend the meeting.

The First Formal Meeting

The president of the day, John Lamont of Liverpool, invited Emma Hardinge Britten to give the invocation and announced that speeches would be limited to ten minutes each. There were so many hundreds of letters that the correspondence could not be dealt with in detail. The First Resolution: "That this assembly considers an annual movable Conference of the Spiritualists of Great Britain and Ireland is a necessity of the present position of importance of our movement" was put by J.J. Morse, seconded by Dr Britten and passed unanimously as a motion with acclamation. During the afternoon session, when numbers increased, Mrs Emma Harding Britten put the resolution (No.3) : "That the time has come for greater unanimity of opinion concerning the fundamental basis of our philosophy, so that the terms Spiritualism and Spiritualist may be associated with an accepted and definite significance."

During her submission, Emma Harding Britten stated that she "could not then transcend the summary of the religious faith her spirit friends had given her when she had to lay the foundation stone of the Oldham Spiritual Temple - namely, that religion consisted in the doctrines of :-

The Fatherhood of God
The Brotherhood of Man
The Immortality of the Soul
Personal Responsibility

Compensation and Retribution hereafter for all the good or evil deeds done here and a path of eternal progress open to every human soul that wills to tread it by the path of eternal good."

This was a vital inclusion for these would later become our Seven Principles.

She went on to say Modern Spiritualism with its religious affirmations of scientific demonstrations stood alone, and therefore she asked that it should neither be affiliated with man-made creeds, labelled with simply human beliefs, opinions or unproved revelation, not be confounded with any sect in existence that did not offer similar and equally incontrovertible proofs of a super-mundane origin and development.

Mr. Newton of Leeds took honour in seconding this resolution and Mr. Kitson led the many Spiritualists eager to speak on behalf of the acceptance (reported July 25th, 1890 'Two Worlds').-

The speeches were of a high and enthusiastic order. So many there had waited years for this opportunity.

Rejoice The Work Awaits!

What a fantastic occasion that must have been. Manchester closed down all local meetings and circles so that no Spiritualist

18

need miss the evening session. There was singing, dancing and many impromptu speeches given that evening. The editor of the Two Worlds made sure that the whole Conference was reported in detail, even though spread over three or four issues. It would be a number of years before Rules and Regulations took a prominent part in Conference. The inaugural Council were asked to arrange next year's meeting at Bradford and no plans were made for any interim activity. How could those, who attended that historic meeting, realise that they were the pioneers of what would become known as the Spiritualist National Union? The largest, the main body of Spiritualists in Britain. How could these people who agreed to serve and support know how their new organisation would grow and even change the concept of Spiritualism in Britain?

CHAPTER 3

PROGRESS THROUGH THE YEARS

There was not much formal work done by the Council that first year. They had not received a mandate from the members, but they did do their level best to spread the word among all the groups, both small and large. The thought of national organisation was not yet general; at first it was just a few inspired individuals who recognised the potential benefit. The next year in Bradford, forty-two Societies chose to affiliate with the Federation. A call went out to encourage individual participation for, although the original concept had been for a Union of Churches, it was soon realised that individuals had much to offer. Also, not all people belonged to one church; mediums in particular, then as now, often worked in a number of churches and found themselves unable to offer one Church their undivided attention. The Council were doing their best. Even so, such are the vagaries of human nature that rumours of favouritism started to circulate. By 1892 Mr Tetlow, the secretary, felt it necessary to make a public announcement in the'Two Worlds' to refute accusations that the Federation had been instituted for the benefit of the few. He stated that:- The Federation is based on unity, freedom and brotherly helpfulness... for the common good of all and not for the isolation and idolation of anyone - all and each of us to be servants to one another, He then appealed for more voluntary workers and warned that the right to vote would be lost if affiliation fees were not paid.

The Federation was desperately short of money, having only £10 in the bank. Some things never change! The need for money has dogged our organisation throughout its short history. We have more resources now but everything is more expensive. Just think, the average cost then per meeting was 12s.6d. (62½p).

Most of the work undertaken by the earlier Council was for the promotion of Spiritualism through missionary work, propaganda meetings, arranging speakers for member societies and distributing informative leaflets. Even with all the work being done on a voluntary basis, some expenses were incurred. Some further form of income was a vital necessity. Every Associate member and each Church in Affiliation paid a yearly subscription, but this was inadequate. It was in 1893, with Mr Peter Lee presiding, that the members passed a motion accepting the principle of Capitation Tax: each Church would be asked for a certain sum per full member to be paid each year. This sum to be 1s.0d. (5p) per member and was optional. The reason it was optional was because societies already paid 12s. 0d. (60p) and associates 2s.6d. (12½p). Most groups recognised the valid need of the organisation although quite a few were worried; they thought they might lose membership if two payments had to be made. The very next year this subject caused tremendous unrest and much heated discussion, which dominated Conference. A motion had been put that would result in the associates losing their right to vote. The societies, who paid more in ratio, only had the right of two votes and they thought this was unfair; they did not see why the Associates should have an unfair advantage. Individuals argued that the Federation was instituted for Spiritualists, not just societies, and they demanded the continued right to vote. The motion was lost. Whether this was because of the discussions, or for financial consideration, is lost to posterity. Many associates had withheld their fees because they feared exclusion from voting rights. This proved to be a substantial loss of revenue. Now that their vote was assured, they would pay up. Our associates, today's Class 'B' members, still have that vital right and have a powerful voice in the running of the Union.

The Federation had survived the first four years. It was time for celebration. Over five hundred people joined the procession through Darwen on Saturday June 30th 1894. Three pretty young Lyceumists carried flowers beneath a splendid new banner. The "Pick up Prize Band" led the Lyceum children, Spiritualists and visitors. Carriages provided for those unable to walk the distance bowled gaily along in front of the Blackburn Lyceumists, members and friends. Then came the Darwen Temperance Society Band. An open lorry at the rear provided a welcome lift for any children who became tired. Hundreds of spectators rallied to see this procession. The picture, reported later in the 'Two Worlds' conveys a feeling of adventure, gaiety and union. Much needed in those days of persecution and uncertainty! Most committed Spiritualists needed courage to declare themselves in the face of continuous opposition. . They were comparatively few in numbers. Thank God that they were also dedicated and strong.

Only four years old and already the fact that they were not empowered to hold property was proving a disadvantage to growth. Mr Johnson pointed out that Halls have been lost to societies after they had subscribed to build them. He proposed that the Executive should obtain a copy of the Wesleyan Poll Deed and should take legal advice with the idea of producing something similar for Spiritualists. He pointed out that we were not yet free from persecution and cited a recent case where the Leeds Sunday Society had been fined two hundred pounds . Mr J.J. Morse then put these suggestions as a resolution: 'that model drafts of .... such necessary deed or deeds should be drawn up by a legal man and submitted to the next Conference'.

Delays and Procrastination

Alas, there loomed the fatal flaw! Lack of money! The work was not completed and the Executive had to admit this. An appeal, the Legal Status Fund, was launched by Mr Todd to finance the necessary work. But it was not until 1897 in Blackburn that the model draft deeds were presented to, and promptly rejected by, the members. The real problem lay in the fact that so many of the members disliked the idea of regimentation. If legal rights were to be secured, it was necessary to declare a set belief. At this time, far more so than now, Spiritualists beliefs differed quite drastically from place to place. Each society had developed according to their own understanding and had come together into organisation with their own ideas already formulated. There was no traditional dogma other than a belief in

22

survival after death. Individual interpretation of religious philosophy did not always coincide and few were willing to forego their ideas in favour of someone else's. Another even larger obstacle was the legal requirement of a governing body. The members had accepted an Executive Council, but baulked at this further extension of power. Fears of oligarchy were revived.

In 1898 a new form of Deed Poll was presented. The discussion on this took up so much time that a further meeting had to be convened so that everyone could have their say. Then, at Southport, in September, the Deed Poll was finally agreed, accepted....it was then lost! At least, according to the records. The whole subject was peculiarly allowed to drop, until at Conference in 1900, the President reported that he could not present the Deed to the Assembly because it was incomplete. Mr. E. Wallis started the questions: 'Where was the original? It was complete at Southport where it had been agreed; where was it now?' Amidst much embarrassment an explanation was given: 'It had been lost in the post'. It turned out that no-one had known where to send the Deed for registration and it had, presumably, been sent backward and forward, to and fro, eventually disappearing in transit. A promise to expedite the matter as quickly as possible was given and the complete Deed Poll was published in the 'Two Worlds' in January 1901. It was subsequently described as 'More a Memorandum of Association, Articles of Association and bye-laws of a company' This was a very accurate description. Subject to further amendments it was accepted by the members at Conference that year.

Many Paths

The work of the Federation was vital to the future of Spiritualism and formed a solid basis for the transition to the new status of Union. Many foundation stones were laid. Not without difficulty and argument. Our pioneers were men and women of principle and strong feelings. They were not afraid to let others know when they disagreed. They were not afraid to stand up and be counted. During their few years of existence they had carried the idea of National Organisation from an ideal to a reality. One of the most vital agreements made was the definite decision not to become another break away branch of Christianity, but to fight for our separate and specific identity. People were ready in numbers for commitment to a new religion of Reason, based on provable fact rather than ancient superstition. A religion of equal opportunity rather than traditional servitude; A religion of the future, not the past. A religion open to all men and women no matter what their race or inherited creed. A Brotherhood of Man in relation with the Fatherhood of God. They were ready for the next big step.

The Transition

In February 1901 an interim conference was held in Blackpool. After a year of hard work and many meetings to discuss the legal position of the Federation, it was now time to put the results of those meetings to the members. The new Deed Poll had been published in the 'Two Worlds' but had not yet been agreed. This then was the main business of the Meeting. The members agreed, after much discussion, alteration and amendments to the Memorandum and Articles of Association. They wanted the Seven Principles incorporated into the memorandum to set out the belief of National Spiritualism in its general form. Their future stability was paramount in their minds. The most important matter at that meeting was the resolution to make it possible for the Federation to gain legal security for holding property. Mr. Bateman, of Tallent Bateman and Thwaites, Solicitors, Manchester, was appointed to act for the Federation in this.

At the Surrey Music Hall in Manchester on the first Saturday in July, Mr Venables, the President, opened the proceedings. After the minutes of the interim Conference at Blackpool had been agreed, Mr Will Philips proposed that a copy of the proposed Memorandum and Draft of Association should be signed by the President and the Solicitor and pasted into the Minutes Book. No- one wanted these records to go astray! Prior to strongly recommending the Lyceum Union to the members, stating that our first duty should be to Lyceum work, he warned that all was not well with their plans agreed at Blackpool.

24

Sensibly, he did not expand on this, but recommended the superior knowledge of Mr. Bateman, who would outline the legalities. He continued to state that: "The Executive had no thought but for the best interest of the movement". Mr Bateman spoke to Conference on Sunday morning. During a long talk upon the constitution he regretted to report that the Board of Trade refused to sanction the registration of the Federation with the word 'Limited' affixed. He had consulted with the Executive and put the alternative possibilities. These were that an unlimited company could be formed or a subsidiary company within the Federation. On the Sunday morning, Mr J.J. Morse on behalf of the Executive, proposed: "That this Conference adopt the advice of Mr. Bateman that the Federation be incorporated under the Joint Stock Companies Act, with liability limited under guarantee, under the style of 'The Spiritualist National Union Ltd'". Mr Johnson seconded, remarking that he "thought this the best scheme possible."

And with these few words our future was decided. Not without argument. Some regretted the need for legality, feeling, in the words of Mr Kenworthy ...that the work to which we are set is entirely in antagonism to the principle of legal status.....the only law which could help the movement was the law of love, and it was only by its observance they could hope to succeed in their mission. Mr Hanson Hey pointed out that we lived in a material world, and must use the material tools in their building. No pun, I think, was intended!

Time Is Not Always Of The Essence
In spite of the serious implications of this vital conference, time was given for that ingredient of love and caring. At two points in the meeting upon reports of serious illness, one, Mr Smedley of Belper and the other the Rev. Chas Ware of Exeter on each occasion Conference was interrupted and some-one dispatched to send a telegraph offering sympathy and cheer. Mr Smedley actually rallied sufficiently to wire back and thank the members for their good wishes. It is in little acts of this nature that our Union has its roots, its strength and its difference. We

are from 'the people, by the people and for the people'. This must be remembered, fought for and perpetuated.

One of the most important, vital aspects of Spiritualism is the ability to recognise the need for change. We pride ourselves upon being a living religion. As individuals learn, so they develop. We as an organisation had learnt valuable lessons in a few short years. As an organisation we could not develop under the Constitution of the Federation. Our aims and objects remained basically the same, but greater legal status was necessary.

The last meetings of members under the title the 'National Federation of Spiritualists' was engaged mainly in agreeing the Articles of Association for the Union. They were discussed at length and in detail. The subject of the qualifying of exponents took up a good proportion of the time. They must not only be passed as proficient by the Exponent's sub-committee, they must be of good moral character....must possess and exhibit earnestness in research, study and exposition in and of Spiritualist philosophy, as well as love of service and devotion to the Spiritualist cause.... They were also required to be of average education. A wonderful, complete assessment of the ideal medium! We still aim for that sort of standard today. The right of Appeal to Conference was agreed at this stage. Although not often used, this right is still ours. It is vital to our freedom of democracy that even the decision of the NEC can be brought before members in General meeting. The question of ownership of property was debated. Representatives declared that many were unsure of their rights and wanted clarification. Some were under the misapprehension that if they sent a rep to Conference then the property they held would become forfeit to the Union. Mr Bateman emphatically denied this on behalf of the Executive. He stated that A society could hand over the Trust to the new formation of the Federation, namely the Union, so that the property could be protected in perpetuity, but this was a matter to be settled by the individual societies. There was no compulsion.

A Rose By Any Other Name

At 8pm on Saturday evening the meeting was adjourned. Those who had indicated that they wished to continue as members under the new regulations of the Spiritualist National Union then recommended the meeting under that banner; seventy-nine, the complement present, had already enrolled as ordinary members. The draft bye-laws just approved by the Federation Conference were adopted with no further discussion; the Officers of the Federation were confirmed to continue as the first Officers of the Union; an invitation to hold the next Conference at Keighly accepted; under the new constitution this would be known as an Annual General Meeting. The president, Mr Johnson, known as "Lancashire Sledgehammer", read a message of fraternal greetings and congratulations from Mrs Cadwallader and the Philadelphia Association. He then brought the meeting to an amicable conclusion, a baby who had achieved the tools of the material world to add to the strength of the Spiritual worlds. A baby whose 100th birthday we celebrate this year 1990.

CHAPTER 4

THE SPIRITUALIST NATIONAL UNION

Mr. W. Johnson had been elected as President to oversee the transition from Federation to Union and to lead the members through any and every teething problem that might arise from the change in status. No easy task! The members Had discussed the new Memorandum and Articles together with the bye-laws required to put these into effect. These were the legal tools necessary to run the organisation and they had eventually been agreed. This did not mean that everyone agreed with everything. Mr. Johnson and his Council soon faced severe criticism. Societies were very worried because legally they could not be part of the Union. In Law only individuals could hold a share; the Churches could not. It had been fully discussed and explained at Conference that the Churches would lose nothing. Their rights would not diminish and they would be represented as part of the Company through their accredited delegates; they were and would remain a vital part of the Union. Unfortunately not all were at Conference to hear this and not all who heard understood and were able to explain to their local body exactly what had happened.A great deal of work and extensive explanation was needed to dispel these very valid fears and to calm the resulting unrest within the ranks.

A lot of time and trouble had gone into making provision in the bye-laws for mediums to be assessed before receiving certification.This move had been made to try to control and improve the quality of the exponents now working for and speaking on behalf of the Union. It was not popular! Many saw the move as an imposition, likely to cause a limitation to the spontaneity of the medium. Even the 'Two Worlds', a journal which had always supported the Union, passed adverse remarks on the advertise-

28

ment placed in its pages promoting the need for applicants for certification. The concept of qualifying the standard of mediumship presented was excellent. Over the years it has been expanded and improvements have been made; they will continue to be made. It was a long time though before it became generally accepted. Even now there are a few who do not believe in the principle of qualification. There are many now, as then, who state openly that A piece of paper will not make a better medium, without acknowledging that the work and effort going into achieving the standard required for 'that piece of paper' can and does improve the individual. I am sure that those who compiled the first lists of qualified workers in 1902 would be gratified to see just how long the present lists are.

Everyone had looked forward to the first full meeting of the Spiritualist National Union because they saw it as a new opportunity. The legal work which had dominated the last few Conferences had been completed; the bye-laws provided for a Consultative Conference to follow after the business meeting, now called an 'Annual General Meeting', most felt that they could concentrate on being Spiritualists again. At Keighly, thanks to the firm tactics and expertise in chairing of 'Sledgehammer' Johnson, the business was indeed completed on the Saturday, leaving plenty of time for discussion, debate and listening to others on the Sunday. Every one thought that this was going to be the pattern for the future. They considered that all the legal wrangling was over and only formal business, which would be minimal, remained.

A little of this optimism was justified; the members had done a very thorough job when going through the new regulations. Naturally there would be changes and additions needed, but the basis was there. Slowly the membership of the Union grew, not however without problems. The scheme for certification continued to be a bone of contention. In 1904 the members of the Lancashire Mediums Union, affiliated to the Spiritualist National Union, passed a resolution not to make application "at present". Most of those who had to book mediums, the Churches, supported the scheme; they could see the sense in setting a standard and showing which wor-

kers achieved that standard. Many churches actually advertised that they would book "only certificated mediums". For
a while this brought matters to a head, but the furore gradually died down and happily the following year the N. E.
Lancashire Union pledged their support for the scheme. It
was still not over-popular but having been successfully established would gradually grow and be accepted.

The necessary work of consolidating the position of the
Union legally went on behind the scenes. By 1905 Tallent and
Bateman, the Unions legal advisers, had drawn up a preliminary Model Trust Deed. Although the Federation had changed
status and name primarily to act as a Trust Company, many of
the Trusts being used were dubious and did not afford the
protection societies needed. The Deed was discussed at length
and referred back to the Council for improvement. Not all
business was of a legal nature. At the close of this A.G.M. cards
were circulated advertising a Spiritualist journal on one side
with the picture and name of the just-elected president, John
Adams. Indignant questions were asked about this at the next
A.G.M. But it was not revealed whether the journal had just
taken a chance on the results, or had separate cards printed for
all eventualities. Certainly they did not try it again!

The Midlands and North continued to be the stronghold of
the organisation, but support was growing in the South. The first
London A.G.M. took place in 1906. John Adams, the President,
supported a suggestion that the country should be divided into
District Councils. Naturally, the Council had discussed the
benefits of this scheme and the London District was the first to
be created as a District Council. Quite a lot of bad publicity had
been given to fraudulent mediums using the cover of the dark-
ened seance room to cheat. To try to overcome this possibility a
motion was passed deploring seances held in the dark, as this
could lead to suggestion of fraud even when there was none.
Many people felt that this was impractical as the conditions
were vital to the production of ectoplasm. Several instances of
mediums producing phenomena in the light were quoted, the
most famous being D.D.Home who, according to Sir Wllm.
Crookes, had refused to work in the dark. The motion was

passed. But generally only mental mediumship is demonstrated in lighted conditions.

The question of social injustice had long been of interest to Spiritualists and 1906 saw the support of two vital issues. One was of particular interest to the Spiritualist and called for education to be secular and taken from the control of the Church. The other was the concern with a scheme for Old Age Pensions to be introduced and the Poor Rate done away with. The old should be able to rest assured of enough income to free them from the fear of the workhouse. Spiritualists advocated a national scheme as opposed to the local arrangements then in force, which often depended on the benevolence, or otherwise, of the Town Council. The Fund of Benevolence has always tried to help those elderly Spiritualists who were sick or in need but they were very limited by lack of money.

It was not until 1909 that Mr Hanson Hey, Secretary to the Spiritualist Nationalist Union, could publicly rejoice in the introduction of the Old Age Pension Scheme which he personally had been working for over the past twenty years. The scheme was almost as he had outlined in an article printed some seventeen years previously. Although he did, in the same New Year speech, printed in the 'Two Worlds' Magazine, regret that so many Lyceumists had abandoned Spiritualism to work for social reform. I feel sure that those who did this chose their priorities as they felt right at the time. We must be proud that so many, trained in Spiritualism, saw a duty to their fellow man and regret that they could not combine the two. In this age of acceptance it is difficult to realise that the Spiritualist was generally viewed with suspicion. In that year the Union was asked to find out what the Spiritualist position was in regard to their funeral rights. Several had been refused permission to hold their own service. The Buried law Amendment Act drafted in 1880 by Gladstone gave the right of equality to every religion, provided the ceremony is a lawful, orderly and Christian one. Correspondence with Archbishops Lang, the Home Secretary, Mr Gladstone and other M.P.s failed to obtain a ruling. Mr Gladstone replied,'It is a question of interpretation'. He was unable to interpret (determine). The Spiritualist National Union determined to fight for the same rights as Jews and Mohammedan to bury our loved ones. Spiritualism was not yet acceptable in Spiritualism.

Towards the end of 1910 and at Conference in 1911, the possibility of England going to war was discussed. A motion was put that '.....this meeting regards with sincere approval the efforts now directed to the maintenance of peace between nations and cordially welcomes the TAFT-Grey proposal as a valuable contribution to that end'. Another motion proposed that we identify with the English Society of Peace. It is not surprising that these proposals were accepted. The physical body is only a temporary home, to be sure, but many regarded premature death as being harmful to the surviving personality, albeit temporarily. More important was the spiritual harm done through the act of one person hating and killing another. Very little was done apart from the passing of these resolutions. The subject made members uneasy - that they would have to face it was not yet certain.

The following year, 1912, William T. Stead passed from this life in that tragic disaster, the sinking of the Titanic. An avid champion of Spiritualism, editor, publicist and medium, he was a great loss and tribute was paid at Conference.

After Conference, on the Monday, Sir Oliver Lodge arranged a tour of the Birmingham University. He too had been praised for the stalwart work he had done on behalf of Spiritualism during the President's address.

The First World War

In 1914, the year that war was declared, Conference debated Capital punishment (abolishment), Suffragettes (forced feeding), the increase of the Blasphemy Laws (deportation of trade union leaders etc.) and an educational centre. No mention of war and little of peace was officially discussed. No motion concerning the war had been tabled! The problem was that Spiritualists were divided. . The Council had promoted no Spiritualist policy at that time; it was left to each individual to take personal responsibility for their actions. Many responded to the patriotic instinct; a minority resisted all efforts and held to the Spiritualist premise that war is against all that is good. The Lyceumists in particular held this view and actively encouraged non-participation. They issued credentials to the Conscientious Objectors.It is difficult now to realise just how the country had responded to the call to arms. 'Your Country Needs You!' Any-one resisting that message wasconsidered unpatriotic, a coward! The Conscientious Objectors were not at first recognised. They were put into prison and some forcibly enrolled into the army where they underwent almost continuous punishment for refusing duties. Many Spiritualist chose to fight. They were after all defending their brothers in Europe from the overwhelming strength of the German armies and ultimately, defending their own country's right to freedom. A Roll of Honour was published in the 'Two Worlds' . An appeal was launched again through the 'Two Worlds', and over £900 was collected, some from abroad, to purchase six ambulances for the troops.

With so many men conscripted many societies were forced to close. Interest in Spiritualism however grew to great proportions. Unfortunately this interest encouraged those who were only wanting to make a profit. There had always been fraudulent mediums. Many articles had been published in Spiritualist journals warning of these dangers. With so many anxious for a last comforting message from those who had died so far from their homes, hundreds of charlatans set up in business. It is not difficult to fool someone who is so willing to believe that they have another chance to say goodbye. These poor souls grasped at any crumb true or false. The word 'Spiritualist' is not exclusive to Spiritualism. The Union had found that out in 1910 when a Motion was tabled 'Irregular Meeting Places' on behalf of the Manchester District Council. The members were concerned then about the practices of people desiring only to make money from psychic phenomena, those not always considered genuine. Legal enquiries showed that the Union could not close these meetings unless a private prosecution was instigated against each one separately.

It was perhaps inevitable that public outrage manifested against the Spiritualist organisation. Papers spoke out against 'harpies of humanity trading upon the mental crucifixion of those whose loved ones have fallen to die upon the wasted fields of France and Flanders'. (The Umpire, August 1916). Hard, harsh, emotive words with a basis of truth. The wrath of the people was vented on the fraudulent and the genuine alike. How were they, who had no previous experience, to tell the difference? Some protection was afforded to Affiliated Churches because they were recognised by the Law, but not to mediums; they were not! A medium taking a service at Longsight Manchester was charged with fortune-telling. Cases where mediums were refused work because of their beliefs were reported. At Conference that year the subject was debated. A motion was put that the Executive Council be instructed to start a fund to finance efforts to effect amendment to the Witchcraft Vagrancy Act. It took over twenty years of hard work for this amendment to be put to Parliament. How many times must Spiritualists have despaired during that time? How many suffered the force of the Law? We who are free must take full advantage of our freedom in true Spiritualist endeavour.

The tide of social and Church vehemence was diminished over the next two years by the public conversion to Spiritualism of several prominent and respected people. Sir Oliver Lodge had for many years been interested in Spiritualism. His book 'Raymond' reported in detail the many evidential messages he had received from his son since he had died in France. Many people thought that it was the evidence given of his son's survival which convinced him of life after death. This is not so; he first stated his conviction publicly in 1907. But it was the book that excited a wider attention. When Sir Arthur Conan Doyle announced his conversion the following year, 1916, even more interest was given. Sir Arthur was well known, of course, for his famous books about Sherlock Holmes. He and his wife allied themselves to the cause and in 1918 became active Spiritualist missionaries. He was the principal speaker at the Conference in Sheffield that year. Once he had started campaigning he put the whole of his energies to the task, often taking as many as five meetings a week. Once again Spiritualism was the centre of attention from the Press, this time on a positive vein. Many more societies affiliated to the Union. Public appeals were made in 'Two Worlds' in 1918 for members to contribute to the Witchcraft Fund and it was suggested that it be called a Parliamentary Fund. In November that year the Armistice was signed and all rejoiced.

The end of the fighting had been predicted in the book 'Private Dowding', published in 1917. It was one of the best predictions of the war.

After the War was Over

There were so many thousands left bereaved, so many in need, not of an empty promise that their loved ones were safe in the arms of Jesus, but that they still existed. That they went on and above all, were able to send back that last message of love and farewell. Spiritualism gave them this second chance and so gained thousands of adherents. Some drifted in out of need and with that need satisfied left. Many stayed to become members. Conan Doyle proved to be one of the most tireless workers in the Union. From 1914 to 1919 the number of societies rose from a hundred and forty-five to three hundred and nine. A mass meeting held at the Royal Albert Hall was considered to be very successful and Conference reported that a profit of £64 was made.

The passing of J.J. Morse in 1919 was deeply felt. He was one of the most distinguished trance speakers the Union had known. He was also a very powerful physical medium. He had worked hard for the organisation, being the editor of the 'Two Worlds' for many years. Through this, his support was invaluable. He continued the custom of donating space regularly in the journal for Union news, space that the Union could not possibly have afforded and which meant that members were kept up-to-date with all the news.

This rapid expansion of Spiritualism gave rise to the subject matter of the Lambeth Conference in 1920, when the State Church debated the facts of modern psychic phenomena. It also possibly precipitated the resignation of that stalwart of the movement, for many years the Secretary, Hanson Hey. For years he had worked tirelessly on behalf of the organisation. His addresses, so often published in the 'Two Worlds' were master-pieces of knowledge, wit and humour. He was greatly loved and appreciated and would be sadly missed.

The legal limitation of churches taking their rightful place in the Union was solved in 1921 when the Memorandum and Articles were finally accepted. The war had delayed much of the business of the Union and much of the 1919 Conference in Nottingham was taken up by agreeing in principle the new Memorandum and Articles of Association. They laid down that subscriptions of Societies were to be 'per capita' of members. This meant that every church member was a member of the Union and had the right to instruct their representative how to vote at district and national meetings. This was good news for the future democratic procedure of the organisation. Only a few churches failed to accept the new conditions, that a Roll Book with the Seven Principles inscribed in the front should be brought into use and that two classes of members should be adopted. One to be full members with voting rights and the other probationary membership for those investigating and not yet committed. Churches were also advised to put 'National Spiritualist' in front of their title to distinguish it from the many other societies who were not connected with the S.N.U. By now there were groups prefixing Spiritualism, not just with Christian titles but also Jewish. Identity had not seemed important at first. Each church knew who they were and membership tended to increase slowly; this gave the newcomer the chance to absorb knowledge and identity from the established congregation. But recent events had shown that this was no longer satisfactory. There had been an influx of members and there were more churches preaching a completely different philosophy to that of the Union.The South of England was still the weakest area of the Union, with few churches choosing to affiliate.

Gradually, however, more and more groups recognised the need for strength in unity. There were so many difficulties in those days for the committed Spiritualist. Many were ostra-cised, lost the chance of promotion, even their jobs if people realised that they were Spiritualists.

CHAPTER 5

PROBLEMS ABOUND

A Woman for President

It was in 1923 that the Union elected for the first time a woman to preside in office. Jessie Greenwood rose to power in a year that highlighted our lack of status as an accepted religion. Scotland refused to regularise our marriage service and our rights of burial were often denied. It was as far back as 1910 that Hansen Hey stated at Conference that he had written to the Right honourable Winston Churchill, who had been most helpful and had directed him to the local Government Board in reference to this matter. He had protested that 'If a fair share of taxes is demanded of us while we are alive, then a fair share of justice should be done to our bodies when we are dead' This form of injustice showed clearly that although legally recognised, we were not accepted. Our mediums still risked prosecution if they practised as mediums. Some had actually been stoned in the street by Christian factions outraged by the communion with Spirit by anyone other than priest. Churches faced fines and or closure by allowing the medium to fulfil their proper function: proving survival.

A petition was started to present to Parliament requiring the protection of our mediums. On legal advice, that the petition would be useless unless it was substantiated by a Bill to achieve our true religious freedom. Council was instructed to prepare a Bill to put to Parliament. This Bill was not presented until 5th April 1926. Over 48,000 had signed the petition which accompanied it and Sir Gerald B. Hurst K.C. was instrumental in the presentation to Parliament.

In 1927 the farthing, found in a F.O.B. collection and mounted to be used for many years as the president's badge, was replaced. Mr Richardson of York presented a new enamel and gilt badge. This was a very generous gesture and was appreciated by the members. The 'Farthing' was honorably retired, but like so many historic objects of the Union's past, I have not been able to trace its present where-abouts.

For many years Sir Arther Conan Doyle had campaigned on behalf of the S.N.U. He had declared publicly that Spiritualism was the basis of all religious belief. His open conversion to Spiritualism had done much to lend credibility to the organisation. He and Lady Doyle regularly attended Conference. Yet in 1927 he tabled a motion that would eventually have repercussions in Spiritualism that have not been fully resolved today. The motion advocated the adoption of a Christian ideal as our own. It excited so much discussion, the President pointing out that we had always resisted the adoption of the extra Principle which would effectively limit our ideology to those people raised within that concept, and exclude those who were opposed to Christianity. No vote was taken at that meeting, but the matter was referred back to the Council for their report to be given at the next A.G.M. The motion was defeated in 1928 with only ten people dissenting the Council report against adoption. It would be untrue to suggest that this motion alone caused a split in Spiritualism. But it did highlight the need to state clearly our identity. In one sense that had always been the case. In a country that has a State religion, it is taken for granted that everyone belongs to that persuasion unless they state otherwise. The Jewish people did not have to state their difference, as their religion is synonymous with their race. The Hindu and the Moslem have similar distinction. But Spiritualism did not have such a great difference and many Spiritualist came from a Christian background; some brought their old habits with them without even thinking about it. Those who objected were often called bigots. Only half the established societies had ever affiliated to National Spiritualism, and many of those were Christian based. From one of these emerged a leader, Winnifred Moyes. Miss Moyes had never investigated Spiritualism and felt that it was 'dangerous to meddle with evil spirits'. But she was convinced that her voices and visions were associated with Christ and that her guide, Zodiac, was associated with Jesus.

The Greater World Christian Spiritualist League, started in 1931, proved to be the strongest rival the Union has had. To date Miss Moyes wanted nothing to do with National Spiritualism as that organisation would not recognise the Christian principle. By 1935 they had an almost equal number of affiliated churches, over five hundred. Some figures show that they had even more than the Union at that time, although like the Union their numbers diminished after this peak.

Conan Doyle accepted the defeat of his motion and continued what had become his life's work,the promotion and advancement of Spiritualism. In 1929 he, together with Ernest Oaten and Estelle Stead had lobbied the parliamentary leaders to promote the Bill. At last in July 1930 they were granted an interview with the Home Secretary. The deputation was led by Sir Arthur, but he was unable to speak more than a few sentences. By this time he was seriously ill; close indeed to his passing six days after. Mr Oaten laid the case supported by Hannen Swaffer, Mrs Champion de Grespigny and the Rev Drayton Thomas. Mr Clynes assured them that the government supported religious freedom for everyone and would give a sympathetic hearing when the Bill was presented. He also advised the Union on changes needed to the draft Bill which would give it a greater chance of success. He hoped that all the different organisations would work together to provide a central body to qualify mediums. He commended the work started by the Union in this direction.

That year a Memorial Service was held at the Royal Albert Hall on November 9th for Conan Doyle.. The speakers were- Miss Lind-Af- Hageby, Ernest Oaten, Rev Drayton Thomas, Estelle Roberts, Hannen Swaffer and Graham Moffat. An empty seat was left for Sir Arthur next to his wife. Many national daily papers reported the meeting ,citing the extraordinary evidence given by medium Mrs Roberts and wondering that Conan Doyle should so clearly have shown that he was present in spirit. Perhaps they would not have reported the meeting in such detail if it had not been honouring a famous man, known not only to the academic, but through his popular novels to the man in the street. Certainly it was of great benefit to the Spiritualist movement as a whole. The fact that such notable people shared the platform and obviously took the demonstration seriously, again helped the cause.

A Time of Trial

Although people like Conan Doyle were honoured by the press and Spiritualism benefited from that approval, mediums in general were still having a bad time of it. Helen Duncan was prosecuted and fined at Edinburgh in May 1933. The trial itself was a farce. The main witnesses for the prosecution lied. It was proved by independent witnesses that they had done so! The evidence against her was contradictory but was accepted. Helen's only defence was that she did not pretend to communicate: she did so! An offer was made to prove, by giving a seance, that Helen was a true medium; this was refused. Ernest Oaten, amongst many others, appeared for the defence to vouch for her honesty. A verdict of 'Not Proven' was brought, but the cost to Mrs. Duncan in stress was great. The members at Conference supported their trust in Helen's mediumship by confirming her certification. Within weeks of the Conference another, lesser known medium was prosecuted in Bristol; she was merely made to pay the costs of the case. The magistrate, Alderman Milton,said that: 'Where there is a Spiritualist church in existence and seances are held, at the moment the law does not interfere'. A very different reaction from that of Edinburgh.

The debate continued about Christian and National Spiritualism. Many advocated a tolerant attitude, but all confirmed their adherence to the concept of National Spiritualism. James McIndoe said at Conference that suggestions had been made that to achieve a unity the Union should compromise. He said 'We have dealt with that matter again and again' and it is our considered conclusion that we cannot add to the principles; the acceptance of which is compulsory before people can become members of our churches. The majority of members did not want compromise, they wanted National Spiritualism.

40

A Psychic Choice

That year, 1933, George Berry retired as General Secretary. A report in the Psychic News states that the Council, faced with over two hundred applicants, invited three or four to be interviewed. Nothing odd in that? they then invited Frank T Blake to psychometrise each one to find the best suited for the job. He actually turned out quite well! Not something that could happen these days, and with the directives to our Churches warning against using psychometry in case of prosecution, just as well. Of course one could argue that it was not done for monetary gain.

Freedom? Not just yet!

The first Reading for "The Spiritualism and Psychic Research (Exemption) Act" was achieved in November. But unhappily at the second Reading it was counted out. Spiritualists were reminded throughout the year that legally they could not even leave money to Spiritualism for the training of mediums. This was because the Law did not recognise mediumship and so anyone disposed to overset such a legacy would be successful. Spiritualists were reminded that their money was needed and there was a form printed so that they could get the right wording for their bequests. This is still printed plainly in the diary for the benefit of the generous.

A questionnaire was submitted to every M.P. in 1935. The manifesto was submitted and signed by Lady Jean Conan Doyle, Hannen Swaffer, J.B. McIndoe (SNU), Mrs B McKenzie (British College of Psychic Science), Mrs St. Clair Stobart (Confraternity of Clergy and Spiritualists), Frank Howburn (Spiritualist Central Council). Mr Aeschimann of the G.W.S.L. declined to sign but later the Greater World did fully support the campaign.The questions asked were varied but they included 'Would you be prepared to support the freedom of Spiritualists to practise their beliefs and would you help to press the BBC to include a Spiritualist service in its programmes? The Rev. Isemonger, Director of the Corporation, had refused so far to allow this. Ernest Oaten did make a recording in 1934 but it was not fully on the religious philosophy. Although the SNU continued to press its case, a further attempt in 1936 also failed. The reason given was that our teaching was not in the mainstream of Christian tradition. We have come far from 1936, but even now fail to secure an acceptance by the National Media of radio and TV as a religion. Even some papers refuse to take our advertisements.

In March 1933, Conan Doyle, through the mediumship of Grace Cooke, started relaying a series of messages. These instances of 'cross correspondence' are often considered to be the best proof of intelligent spirit survival recorded. The alternate circle was in Winnipeg, Canada. Dr Hamilton, of that group, confirmed the significance of the messages and said that they had further tests to make. Sir Arthur, ever propagating our movement on earth, was continuing his task from the spirit realms. Lady Doyle had continued with her support and must have been greatly comforted to know that her dear husband was equally active.

CHAPTER 6

PERSECUTION, PROSECUTION AND PRESENTATION

War or Peace?

In the years leading up to the World War II many messages of warning were given from Spirit. Haig, Kitchener, Jellicoe, they all told of the possibility of European hostility. At Conference in 1933 and in many other meetings, special thoughts of peace were invited. In spite of these warnings two highly respected Spirit friends, Red Cloud, guide of Estelle Roberts and Silver Birch, Maurice Barbanell's guide at Hannen Swaffer's home circle, predicted peace. Prophecies published in the 'Two Worlds' by Dr Wood, called the 'Rosemary Records', proved equally unreliable, although this channel had previously given similar warnings.

When war was declared people were naturally bitterly disappointed; some felt devastated as they had relied on the words of Spirit.These predictions caused uproar in the media, but oddly the mediums were not completely discredited, although no explanation was offered for the seemingly gigantic error of prediction. The Union did point out that the basis of Spiritualist philosophy decried prediction, we are not fortune- tellers. It was much later that the 'predictions' warning about the possibility of war were revealed. A very comprehensive article in the PsychicNews and 'Two Worlds' explained that to publish such predictions at the time, in view of the attempts being made by the government to secure peace, would have been tantamount to treason. For various reasons the movement did go into a decline and has not even now regained the strength or membership of the pre-war years.

During the 1914-18 war many churches were limited in their activities, but this Second World War had a far more drastic effect, particularly in larger towns. The blackout made travelling difficult and evening meetings virtually impossible. Some meeting halls were actually requisitioned for war work and many churches disbanded 'for the duration'. Men were called up and women were required for essential war work. Many mediums had difficulties due to travel restrictions in certain sensitive areas. The Union had already considered the subject of appointing Ministers. In many ways it was against the essence of Spiritualism, which did not want a priesthood. The appointment of Ministers however, would fulfil two functions. One, it conveyed an air of respectability and permanence to the outsider and it would allow an easing of the restrictions placed on travel, particularly in the South. Ministers were not subject to the same rules as the ordinary traveller.

Application was made to the Home Office before passes could be issued. They were in fact a Spiritualist identity certificate and carried the Seal of the Union. They cost one shilling. Efforts were also made to secure the appointment of a Spiritualist Chaplain, to Minister to those Spiritualists already in H.M. Forces. This was refused on the grounds that the numbers of registered Spiritualists did not warrant separate Chaplains. Considerable confusion was caused by the fact that the Minister of Labour, then Ernest Bevin, refused to concede that Spiritualism was a religion or had Ministers of religion. This denial took place within weeks of an appellate tribunal granted exemption to George Darsley, on the grounds that Spiritualism was as much a religion as the Baptist or Methodist religion. Ernest Oaten had been equally confused in 1918 when he was refused exemption by the Sheffield court, but was told by Justice Darlington, on appeal, that he would not have made the same decision.

The question of pacifism was not an easy one. The Lyceum movement supported this without reservation. But the majority of S.N.U.Members supported the statement issued by the Council that'we cannot be unmindful of the fact that peoples of several nations have had their freedom and liberty restricted by brute force; our duty is to assist the weak and suppressed'.

Throughout the war years Spiritualists worked hard in their own areas to keep their churches open, to offer the help and comfort so desperately needed by the bereaved families of the dead. Collections were taken and once again members were asked to contribute to an ambulance fund. By 1942 the Planning Committee, (Hannen Swaffer and Maurice Barbanell both worked on this Committee), were looking to the future. They visualised the time when meetings would be"..taken out of the attics and stables where so many are now held. We must weld the movement into a united body under the banner of progress."

Efforts were still underway to try to amalgamate the Lyceum Union with the Spiritualist National Union, but without success. Due to this lack of agreement, a youth movement was inaugurated to take the place of the Lyceum training. This caused even more bitterness between the two and Mr. Fruin accused the Union of trying to ruin the Lyceums. The youth movement did not make any real progress and was eventually dropped. There was actually an increase in membership that year and then the police started a vicious campaign of prosecution. Using disguise, some as sick soldiers wearing hospital blues, others as grieving relatives, they visited mediums, paid their fee, accused them of fraud and then arrested them. One after another medium was charged with 'claiming to tell fortunes.' Austin Hatcher and Emily Little of Cardiff were imprisoned. Mrs Townsend and Florence Camper were fined. Eleven a healer who claimed to be a minister of religion was fined for failing to comply with directions as to employment.(The law did not recognise Spiritualist ministers). The Union was criticised for not using the Parliamentary Fund money to defend them.

The Law Proves Useful - Union Gets £1,500 Damages

The Union had already had problems with the Parliamentary Fund in 1933. An article, in the International Psychic Gazette, had made the accusation that the Fund was grossly mal-adminstered, never used for the purpose for which it had been publicly subscribed and that no account had been rendered. This was strenuously denied; the Fund was properly audited and accounted for to the members at every A.G.M. But the article was reprinted, this time by the Hillside Press. The Union took court action. John Lewis and C.A. Aeschimann, with Winnifred Moyes of the Hillside Press, equally defended the action. Many side issues were raised during the trial in respect of controversy between S.N.U. and Christian Spiritualism; the history of the Fund and a law case where Mr Oaten resisted the call to Military Service on the grounds that he was a Minister of Religion. Mr Oaten agreed that the costs of that case were paid from the Parliamentary fund. He said that although he was not actually eligible for call-up because of health reasons, the Union had wished to make a point and had asked him to bring a test case, some fifteen years previously, as President of the Union. This was done purely to establish Spiritualism as a religion. Therefore it was quite in order that the case should be paid for out of the Parliamentary Fund. The prosecution felt that it was probably this incident which led to the subsequent libel. During the case it emerged that Lewis had made frequent criticisms of the handling of the Fund since 1924 and Aeschimann became involved, as printer, after the first article appeared, although he had received correspondence about the article from the S.N.U. denying the allegations. He was more concerned with the controversy in the Union and its non-acceptance of the divinity of Jesus Christ, and chose not to believe the denial; he went ahead and printed the article. Because of the correspondence received, this part of the case was considered to be more serious. The jury awarded the Union £1,500. to be divided between the three defendants. After the costs had been paid, the residue of the damages awarded were not used for general but for benevolent purposes. The G.W.C.L. were very angry about the result of this action and it caused an even wider rift between the two organisations. From that time they refused to sit on any committee where the Union was represented. It was many years before the two were to work again together in unity.

Open, But Not All Hours!
The majority of churches during the period of the war had made valiant efforts to keep their doors open. Some had been

forced to close, many had to change their hours of service. The Greater World had suffered too, but was still a very strong movement in the South. Not really the time for domestic upheavals in the Union; but there were. In 1942 the Union was challenged by Mr Fruin, President of the B.S.L.U., for starting the youth movement in opposition to their Lyceums. He accused them of trying to ruin the Lyceums. The Union and the B.S.L.U. still could not come to agreement, although so many Spiritualist worked for both organisations and their aims were so similar. In '39 Mr. Fruin had actually stated that 'After long and careful consideration of the present position endeavouring to judge it from all angles, I have come to a firm conviction that for the progress of both sections it is a mistake to continue with two Unions.' There were many Lyceumists who disagreed with that, they resented the fact that not every Church supported a Lyceum and that the Union had a separate education scheme.

That was not all; Hannen Swaffer challenged the Union to 'get back to fundamentals'. That particular row resulted in 'Swaff' resigning as Honorary Vice-President. At first the Union refused to admit that anything was wrong and it took a long time to resolve the disagreement. Basically it all started with 'Swaff' in that he thought that public worship was overvalued, often useless, and at a meeting of the London District he said so, in no uncertain terms! Ernest Keeling took strong offence and made some rather unfortunate remarks. The argument escalated and the whole facts were not revealed for quite some time, the Union denying that there were any problems and refusing to formally accept the resignation. An article in the 'Two Worlds' and 'Psychic News' revealed all to the members and a further letter printed, from Hannen Swaffer, revealed that he had asked the matter to be kept private until after the A.G.M. Eventually the problem was smoothed over and all settled down. 'Swaff' had not changed his mind, but he was an essentially generous man and had no desire to hurt anyone, particularly within the Movement which he had supported so well and so long.

For years the Union had been criticised for not making more use of Air Chief Marshal, Lord Dowding, who was a noted speaker on behalf of Spiritualism. In 1943 they suddenly woke up to the potential of this valuable propagandist and used his services extensively. He spoke at Conference and at numerous meetings up and down the country. He was asked to be one of the party to present a petition to Parliament demanding our freedom from persecution. The Union was then criticised for 'lionising' the man in preference to other Spiritualists of longer standing. This was a valid point but the Executive knew that they were still not in a very strong position and Lord Dowding had considerable influence in Parliamentary circles. They needed to use people of this quality who had 'clout' with those in power.

Freedom Does Not Come Cheap!

In 1943 yet another Freedom Fund was started. The Union was the Trustee, but several other interested organisations contributed. This was specifically to assist mediums who were being badly harassed by the police in certain parts of the country. Anne Novack was the first medium to have her defence paid by this fund and the Union was strongly criticised for refusing to take her case to Appeal. They said that as there was no hope of winning an Appeal, in that case they declined to waste monies that would be needed for other individuals. Her defence Council, Captain Loseby, spoke at Conference that year addressing the members absentmindedly, as 'members of the jury'! Capt. Loseby was at that time not very experienced at the bar. But he had previously defended mediums, was a Spiritualist and understood the problems of mediumship. He did an excellent job under difficult circumstances and was used extensively by the Union in cases of this type, notably Helen Duncan. It was at his insistence, with Mr. McIndoe, that the Freedom Committee was born, May 28th 1943. A special appeal had raised £5000.

It was a curious anomaly that practice of Spiritualism was considered illegal and yet the Under Secretary of State gave permission for Ministers to visit prisoners who requested their Ministry. A scheme was devised to try to separate the fraudulent mediums from those who were genuine. A National Directory would be compiled which could form a basis of defence; this list was based on those who were certificated. Herbert Morrison offered a concession, in answer to the petition presented to the under Secretary, Osbert Peake: 'There is no question in war-time to introduce legislation to amend section 4 of the Vagrancy Act, but he would instruct the police to prosecute only where a person is an imposter and has taken money'. Not enough, but many small successes would accumulate and become an avalanche.But that would be in the future

Helen Duncan

Once again Helen Duncan was in trouble. She had travelled to Portsmouth to work for two weeks. At the first seance a young sailor materialised and told his mother than his ship, H.M.S. Barham, had been sunk with great loss of life. The horrified woman denied this. She stated that she had not been informed. 'You will be, three weeks from now,' replied her son. The poor woman did not wait, she contacted the Admiralty for information. Two senior Admiralty officials then visited her; they wanted to know where she had received her information. She told them quite openly, never imagining the consequences. At the same seance a warning was given about admitting a man in naval uniform to the next session. This was not noted and neither was a further warning. On 19th January 1944, just as the ectoplasm had started to manifest, the police violently and forcibly interrupted the seance. Helen and three others who had helped organise the meeting were charged the next day under the Vagrants Act. Helen was detained in Holloway prison for five days. It was obvious from the start that this was no ordinary charge and reasonable to suppose that it was connected with the information about the sinking of the Barham. (That news had been withheld from the public for over three weeks) The Chief Constable had been consulted, unusual in itself, and had asked for her to be detained, Bail was refused and the matter was referred to the Director of Public Prosecution.

Even the general public were outraged when, in 1944, Helen Duncan was charged with being a witch. Dozens of people flocked to speak in her defence including Alfred Dodd (author), J W Henries (chief reporter from the Scotsman), Rev Maurice

Elliott and Hannen Swaffer. All to no avail. Helen had already been condemned. Mr Loseby conducted an admirable defence but on April 4 Helen was sentenced to nine months in prison. Mrs Brown had been sentenced to four months and the hosts of the fateful evening, Mr and Mrs Homer, were bound over for two years. Poor Mr and Mrs Homer also suffered the indignity of having their lack of marital status revealed, a subject which was very delicate in those days. Although they had lived together for over a quarter of a century, in the eyes of the law she was Elizabeth Jones and society condemned her for being a 'loose' woman. By September when Helen was released, she had suffered a nightmare of indignity. She travelled home to Scotland, tired and ill, vowing not to work as a medium ever again.

The case of Helen Duncan gave a fresh impetus to the driving need for the amendment of the Vagrancies and Witchcraft Acts. It also brought new support from the public as well as in both Houses. By 1945 a number of Ministers had pledged their help. Ernest Bevin, the Foreign Secretary, said that he wanted an inquiry and P.J. Neil-Baker, the Minister of State, said that it was an anomaly that Spiritualism should be penalised. The association of Canadian Spiritualists wrote in support and urged immediate action. In August, Clement Attlee once again wrote offering his support; he had communicated with the Union as far back as 1935, although he had not been able to offer practical help, only moral commitment.

Naturally, the case of Helen Duncan was discussed at length at the Conference of 1945. Although she had vowed not to resume her work, that was the result of months of worry and ill-treatment in prison.She did start giving seances quite quickly considering the length of her ordeal. The Union wanted to take over the responsibility for overseeing her sittings, not only for Helen's protection, but also for the good name of the organisation. This was refused quite categorically. Members felt this rebuff, particularly as £3,000 from the Freedom Fund had been used in her defence. Many considered that a precedent had been set in the accusation of witchcraft, and that the way was now open for further prosecutions under this more severe category. This debate opened up another important subject; the need for education. One salient point was well made: 'We are anxious that our members should be better informed about Spiritualism and more capable of demonstrating its truths. Our greatest dangers are uninformed emotional enthusiasm and premature mediumship.'

This anxiety about the future was well balanced by the report of the various committees. The Planning Committee were anticipating a tremendous response to the celebration of the Centenary of Modern Spiritualism in 1948. There would be attempts to co- operate with the other main organisations for this event. A Centenary fund had been started in order to pay for the celebrations and the London District were going to try to buy new Headquarters. Mr. McIndoe reported that efforts were being made to re-establish the International Federation which had been forced to discontinue during the War years. The Freedom and Parliamentary Committee had decided to affiliate with the Committee of Civil Liberties and felt that this move would give added strength to their work. Over £5,000 had been received, but this would not be enough and further donations were requested. A motion was carried that all churches should adopt the words 'National Church' in their title. This was another attempt to differentiate from the non-affiliated groups. There was so much to catch up upon now that normality was returning to the country.

Although the Union had previously upheld the work of Helen Duncan, the Education and Exponents Committee had reluctantly agreed that her work had seriously deteriorated since her trial. They withdrew her diploma, stating that they hoped that this would be temporary. The matter would be reviewed as soon as Helen was working up to her normal standards. They had investigated during her physical seances in Lancashire and found lack of adequate control and quality..' The 'Psychic News' echoed this feeling and in August that year printed yet another warning to Helen, stating that if she did not take great care the next sentence would not be nine months but five years. Alas, this prediction fell short of the facts. Helen did regain her former faculties and continued to use them on behalf of those in need. She did, in spite of intolerable ill health, start to travel again and she was further accused by the police, although this time she was not brought to trial. The untimely interruption of a seance in Nottingham caused such injuries that she was hospitalised for a month. Helen Duncan did not recover from this final ordeal. In November, Albert, her faithful and loving control, came one last time to take his medium home.

In 1945 another deputation went to the Home office, where it was received by the Home Secretary. He promised consideration. Six months later he sent a letter stating that 'Any relaxation of the law as it applies to such fraudulent activities would be specially dangerous at this time, when there is such a wide field for the unscrupulous exploitation of personal loss and bereavement.' Such prejudice did not make those wonderful fighters give up. The Freedom and Parliamentary Committee continued their work, drafting a new Bill. They would, and eventually did, win through. The issue was too important to neglect.

CHAPTER 7

WE WIN A BATTLE

United We Stand

In January 1948 the S.N.U. and the B.S.L.U. united into one organisation. There would now be a Lyceum Department of the S.N.U. which would retain control of its own organisation, offices, finances and elections. It would have special responsibilities in the training of the young. This amalgamation was not popular with all the Lyceumists. Many wanted to remain completely separate from the main body. Not all affiliated churches supported Lyceums in spite of many presidential calls to this effect through the years. For a long time the Lyceum Union actually had more members and funds than the Union. Although they used mainly established affiliated church premises for their meetings this was not always the case. Nothing would change in this direction but it was hoped that more churches would encourage and support a Lyceum Group; they, in turn, would support the parent church. This had been the original intention for Lyceums but had not worked out as intended. It was hoped that the amalgamation would be beneficial for both Unions.

Another good thing to come out of 1948 was a rally of various Spiritualist organisations who met at the Kingsway Hall in September that year. Also the three main organisations, the S.N.U., the G.W.C.L. and the Marylebone Spiritualist Alliance, which later changed its name to the S.A.G.B (Spiritualist Association of Great Britain) co-operated to present the Centenary Celebrations of Modern Spiritualism at the Royal Albert Hall. The meeting was a tremendous success, but the truce did not last. By 1949 a resolution was accepted at Conference inviting Spiritualists and Spiritualist organisations who subscribe to the Seven Principles to join the Union. It had been amended deliberately from '..of all shades of theological opinion..' The controversy was again the limitations of accepting the basic tenets of Christianity into a religion which Spirit had intended to be acceptable to all the world, not just those from a Christian background.

Perhaps if we had compromised and changed direction to incorporate Christianity we would have had greater success with our efforts to persuade the BBC to allow our religion air-time. Although the earlier Broadcasts forbade subjects of a controversial nature, Sir William Haley had announced, in 1945, that: 'We are determined to increase the amount of controversial broadcasting in the Home Service' By 1946 even the taboo subject of sex had been tentativel explored; not religion though if it differed from Christianity. Several Rationalists were allowed to explain their dissension but they were well known in other fields; Bertrand Russell, Dr. Julian Huxley and Prof: Gilbert Murray could say why they chose to remain outside a religious persuasion, but our ministers could not explain why they accepted and chose to promote Spiritualism. For some years members had been asked to present a questionnaire to their respective Members of Parliament, effectively asking if they would support our rights of freedom if they were returned. Would they condemn the totalitarian attitude of the BBC? In 1946, a deputation from both Houses of Parliament was received by Haley. They demanded to know why the BBC were adamant in their negative attitude and were told outright: 'We live in a Christian country and are entitled to forbid Broadcasts expressing views not in harmony with the Christian tradition and Creed.' His attitude had not changed one iota!

The End of the Beginning

It is with no shame that I borrow this phrase from Helen Duncan's book. There it indicated her entry into the next phase of her existence; her body worn and tired from the vagaries of life. With the Union it indicates the Bill presented to Parliament late in 1950 and receiving Royal Assent as the Fraudulent Mediums Act in July 1951. At last the law recognised that genuine

mediumship existed. The fraudulent were still liable for prosecution, but the Movement had always tried to police itself.
They hated the fraud just as much as any magistrate. This Act,
which amended the Witchcraft Act of 1735 and section 4 of the
vagrancy Act 1824, effectively extended religious tolerance to
the Spiritualist Movement and gave us a freedom which, although hard won, was very, very satisfying.

The entire movement celebrated. A victory dinner was held
in the Houses of Parliament on Monday July 16th. Special guests
were Air Chief Marshal Lord Dowding, GCB, GCVO, CMG,
who piloted the bill through the House of Lords, and Mr T.J.
Brooks, MBE, JP, MP, who was responsible for its success in the
House of Commons. Because there was business as usual in
Parliament, the Home Secretary and other MP's had to leave on
several occasions to register their vote and this caused some
disruption in the order of the programme of speeches. Mr John
Stewart, Secretary of the Freedom Committee, was the chairman
and he coped splendidly. The first toast of the evening was to
Parliament coupled with the name of the Right Honourable J.
Chuter Ede. The Home Secretary, Mr Clement Davies, KC, MP,
suggested that parliament might not have done Spiritualists a
favour, as persecution often helped a movement. Not meant as
words of doom and certainly not taken that way! Many Spiritualists around the country would certainly have understood
the sentiments but few that might well have agreed with them.
A half-a-century of toil and worry and work was behind them.
There would be time enough tomorrow to gird their loins for
future battles.The war was not yet won.

After the Ball Was Over

After all the excitement of the previous months, even years,
ordinary business seemed just that- ordinary. The Union staff
still had to function on a mundane level and there were problems. The income of this religious body has always been uncertain. The subscription remained the main source of regular
revenue and had never been quite enough to cover running
costs. The special appeals for ambulances during the war, the
Freedom Fund to defend individual mediums and the Par-

liamentary Fund to subsidize our fight for freedom had all been well supported. They appealed to the emotions; running an office did not! Percy Wilson warned the members about the seriousness of our financial position in 1951. We desperately needed a trained accountant who would have to be paid. The secretary was over-burdened; printing cost more, as did paper. Nothing came cheap, except perhaps our religion.

At conference members voted on Saturday declining to authorise a raise in subscriptions of one shilling. On Sunday they were informed that their lunch would cost one shilling extra. No one complained. They paid the one shilling extra for food to fill their stomachs and refused one shilling to support their adopted religion, the food of their souls. We had won a battle; what of the war?

Many people were predicting the beginning of the end, yes, even in the year when we had achieved one of our most important objectives. Percy Wilson, the President, was sure that it was rather the end of our new beginning, but could not help a feeling of despondency. Members had identified with the struggle for freedom, for the individuality of Spiritualism. But many still did not identify with their religion as a national body. Those who did became subscribing members. But there were thousands who although members by virtue of being members of our affiliated churches knew nothing about the Union. Few churches emphasised the responsibility that they had to the organisation, much less that of their members. The past decade had concentrated on a matter of national and future importance for all Spiritualists: that mediums have the right to demonstrate the proof of survival without persecution. Before that the promotion, building and consolidating of the foundations of national organisation occupied the central point of effort. Now should have been the time to establish a solid identity. Unfortunately the Council found that there were still legal problems to be solved. A change in the law necessitated alterations to the constitution of the Union and the Memorandum had to be amended This was completed on the 11th March 1950. In the welter of legalities and the mundane the vital issue of identity was neglected, a golden opportunity missed and problems shelved to be dealt with by future generations.

The next general meeting must now work within the organisation to establish stability. The constitution had been changed to protect the charitable status of the Union and the Council had sought legal help to rectify a number of trust deeds found to be deficient. This matter had been highlighted as more churches chose to use the Sale Trust and Deed, introduced by J. B. McIndoe in 1940, which gave greater protection to churches and was more efficient. Fortunately this did not constitute a problem. The Charity Commissioners were most helpful and the legal status of the Deeds re-established.

The new Model Rules, as they were known at that time, were issued in February 1951. Four thousand copies were printed and sold. A second print run was immediately required to fulfil the orders from churches and members. This was important, because they laid down in detail the basic way each church must comply with the bye-laws in order to stay within the charitable status of the Union. As Percy Wilson stated: "There must be less procrastination; there has been too much leaving it to the Angel World, or to chance". He wanted action for the future and not just working to keeping with the present.

In this, the Diamond Jubilee year of the founding of the S.N.U. and the Golden Jubilee of its incorporation, pronouncement was made on the use of the title 'Reverend' by S.N.U. exponents and severe censure imposed on the use of unauthorised or ambiguous titles.

Members Demand A Spiritual Lead

For too many years the work of the leaders of the S.N.U. had focussed almost exclusively on administration. It had to be. In the circumstances it was right that it should be, but apart from a few motions put to Conference referring to social obligations, no real Spiritualist direction had been issued. When a motion requiring the 'Hierarchy' to accept the responsibility of spiritual leadership, was placed at Conference as a direct result of letters to the 'Two Worlds', Percy Wilson, the former President, was violently against the concept. C. Quastel was in favour; he saw

57

it as a moral duty. He recognised that each soul must make its own struggle towards perfection, but saw that with wise leadership, the way may be shown towards true democracy - spiritual freedom and attainment. Alas, little came of this vital point. In the past, great speakers had filled vast halls and people had listened to their words from Spirit realms; even now this road could have been pursued. Instead, more and more emphasis was laid upon communication used purely to prove survival. There were exceptions. A Spiritualist Council for Common Action had been started in 1957 for the purpose of providing means of organisation for the major Spiritualist organisations. Its objects were simple and practical and it was hoped that they would establish recognition that there is a definite body of Spiritualist opinion which cannot be ignored. Only when unanimous decisions were reached would any action be taken. They co-operated in securing religious rights in the three sections of His Majesty's Services and made representations to Parliament in reference to BBC airtime, and the Ministry of Health to ask for investigation into the handicaps suffered by non-orthodox healers. Little difficulty was found in agreeing matters outside their own philosophies. But the fundamental difference between the two main organisations remained a stumbling block to wholehearted co-operation.

Quastel's Umbrella

Quastel desperately wanted all Spiritualist societies to amalgamate under the aegis of the S.N.U. When he became President in 1958 he was in a better position to promote this idea. It became known as 'Quastel's umbrella' . His ideal was known and respected, but it remained a dream. Even he had stated firmly at Conference that only S.N.U. philosophy should be promoted from S.N.U. platforms. Even he must have realised the impossibility of asking the Christian Spiritualists to renounce their parochial attitude and support National Spiritualism.

Quastel was an idealist who really believed in the possibility of all Spiritualist organisations amalgamating with the S.N.U. This may happen in the future, although it seems as unlikely now as it did then. He did successfully put a resolution to

Conference to introduce a religious basis to the International Spiritualist Federation. The Union representative would take the motion to the next International Congress.

Another organisation had started in 1957, 'The Union of Spiritualist Mediums'. They actually stated in their constitution that there should be no affiliation with any other spiritualist organisation.

The 'National Federation of Spiritual Healers', headed by Harry Edwards, was also challenging the Union at that time in the field of healing. Neither had their own premises, but relied on the use of individual churches and halls to hold meetings and promote their cause. By 1959 this came to dissension and the Union issued a directive to stop the use of their churches by rival organisations. Harry Edwards did not take this lightly. For a while feelings ran high and articles appeared both for and against in the Psychic Press. Not very helpful to Quastell's 'Umbrella' or to the general image presented to the public! The subject was not fully resolved but eventually died down and was allowed to be forgotten.

Don't Use Psychometry

Some members of churches ask even now why can we not use psychometry. At one time it appeared to be acceptable. Indeed one Union secretary was chosen by this means. The truth is that this is one of the areas where the law will still operate under the Vagrancy Act. 'Pretending to tell fortunes'- that is how it is phrased. Due to successful prosecutions brought in the past, there are plenty of precedents. Three such prosecutions were levied in 1955, two under the Vagrancy Act and one under the Fraudulent Mediums Act. Most people were shocked. The consensus of opinion was that the new law had freed mediums from such danger. It had of course given a greater degree of freedom, but for Spiritualist mediums practising a genuine part of their religious philosophy: proving survival. What was not then appreciated was that anything associated with fortune-telling, where payment of any kind was accepted, fell foul of the law. A directive was issued at once from the Union warning churches of the danger. The dangers were obviously not sufficiently emphasised, because few churches ceased their activities in this field, although many confined such meetings to their own members and so minimised the threat.

In 1953 Percy Wilson resigned, not only from Presidency but from Council. He stated that he could not accept the responsibility for the decisions the Council had taken since the last AGM. At the time he had made it clear that he did not see the role of the Council as spiritual advisors to the members for the purpose subscribed. The council should be administrative or legal in character. His years concentrating on the business side of the Union had perhaps blinded him to the original concept of a religious philosophy. He did what he thought was right. His son Lawrence supported this view and also tendered his resignation. Harry Dawson was duly elected to Presidency. In that same year Ernest Keeling condemned the emphasis now laid on academic qualifications. He wanted more attention paid to a person's spiritual qualities. There were many who agreed with him, but instead of working for a compromise each side held to their own ideals, such is human nature!

The truth was that there must be balance . We were far from 'safe' from the law. A list had been compiled of qualified mediums which was to be a basis of protection, but that did not prevent the stupidity and ignorance of individual official action. Once again in 1956 Helen Duncan was manhandled by the Police. Unhappily this was during a physical seance after the ectoplasm had started to flow. Helen had suffered so much stress and ill-health that by November when a further threat of prosecution was sent by the Nottingham Police Constabulary, she was close to her final hours on earth. Soon her pain was to be part of her past and a fine worker would move on to fresh fields and new experience. Our loss, their gain.

CHAPTER 8

A WHITE ELEPHANT

Generous to a Fault

Arthur Findlay is remembered by most of the S.N.U. for his home at Stansted which is now our College of Psychic Studies. This was gifted to the Union in 1964. What is not realised is that he also gave his shares in the Psychic Press to the Union in 1956. He had bought the shares from Maurice Barbanell within one week of the start of the 'Psychic News', when capital was desperately needed. He wanted 'Barbie' to co-edit the ' Psychic News' and the 'Two Worlds'. A charter existed which ensured the continued independence of the 'Psychic News' and that status is still maintained. Unfortunately the Union also ran into financial difficulties in 1962 and had to surrender the shares. At so many conferences members had called for their own paper. It is ironic to realise that we held the controlling interest in what is such a well known weekly psychic journal, even if only for a few years, and yet could not direct the editorial interest. For many years the 'Two Worlds' donated space in their publication to the affairs of the Union. Their editors also sat on Council. Indeed, the Union is now the Trustee of the Two Worlds Publishing Company and the present editor, R. Taylor B.A. is a member of the National Executive Council.

The finances of the Union desperately needed boosting. Hannen Swaffer, still our Honorary Vice-President, made an attempt through the courts to gain control of the Conan Doyle Memorial Fund. This had been started to establish a permanent centre in the West-End of London, but in twenty years had only raised £3,000. This could not possibly be used for the intended purpose. But in the knowledge that Arthur Findlay had deeded Stansted Hall to the Union in 1964, it was reasonable to argue that the Union was in the best position to fulfil the desire of Conan Doyle's widow to establish a permanent centre. The Hall would not be fully transferred until after Mr Findlay passed into Spirit in 1964. Although arrangements had been made by Mr Findlay to provide funds to help run the Hall, it was even then suspected that more would be needed. The membership of the Fund had to be circulated before permission could be given by the courts for change of purpose.

Although the property left by Arthur Findlay was transferred to the Union in 1964, it could not possibly be used for the purpose intended at that time. Apart from necessary structural alterations, rooms, divided to make two or three separate rooms, other more mundane matters had to be dealt with. With one small family living there, waste had been disposed of by means of a cess pit and that had been adequate. Now it was not and a drainage system had to be laid. The electricity had been changed from generator to mains. But again this was inadequate for a building to be used by the public. There were many, even then, who looked upon the new aquisition as a 'white elephant' which should be disposed of as soon as possible. The Council had not jumped at the proposition when first approached by Sir Arthur. The truth was there were not sufficient funds readily available to make the place into a viable part of the Union capable of paying its way. Stansted Hall had been used for some Spiritualist activity in the past. Sir Arthur had held a reception during Centenary Week in 1948 for the International Spiritual-ists Federation. There was an ordination ceremony held in August 1964 by Dr. John Winning. Wilfred Watts, B.A., M.S.N.U, had been the first Minister ordained in Stansted; not in the Sanctuary - that did not exist at the time - but in the lower gallery with the Longton Choir grouped on the stairs. It proved to be convenient for meetings and soon there was a hard core of far-sighted people rooting for the necessary money to be pro-vided for the improvements required. Mr. Gordon Higginson, then the Class B Representative, was one such.

In 1965 the first manager, Tom Harrison, was appointed and by 1966 the college was open for business. An article in the 'Psychic News' labelled it a 'Psychic Hotel'! In fairness to the

'Psychic News' it was advertised as an "educational, convalescent and holiday house".

For a long time members had been concerned about the organisation of the National Council. It had gradually changed over the years and now consisted of two representatives from the eight electoral areas and from the Lyceum Union, plus a Class B representative. The various committees had been formed through necessity and were not always run efficiently. Sometimes meetings went on from friday right through to monday and yet not all the required business was completed. It was said that more business was done outside the meeting than in! This was all very well, but it meant that endless reports had to be compiled and that not everything was done democratically. Some members had numerous jobs, others had none. The Council was the ruling body and was basically top heavy. An attempt was made in 1966 to have the articles altered so that each district council would elect a representative. As it was then, an electoral District might comprise one or two Districts; they had two representatives. The change was opposed on two counts. The Treasurer, Miss Owen, stated that this would lead to even greater expense and the London District felt that it would be very unfair if this method was used when they, with ninety-eight churches would only have the same representation as South-West Lancs, who had only nineteen churches. Needless to say, the motion was lost. In 1966 Tyne-Tees Television came to Stansted Hall to film, and although this caused considerable disruption at the Hall, the resulting publicity seemed to be good for the Union.

Mr Higginson was elected Class B representative and carried on an intensive effort to attract more subscribing members. He also supported, indeed was at the forefront of the general interest now being shown in Stansted as a centre to be used for education. A motion was lost which would have meant that future members of the Executive Council would have to have passed the administration course of the Union, possibly because it would have been difficult to implement such conditions and few on the Council would have qualified. An advisory committee had been set up to consider the implications of the Union's financial situation and general organisation, but after five years had little to show for the time spent. Although membership had increased, so also had expenses. So the Union was still in a very uneasy position.

After the problems with whether the Churches should offer space to the National Federation, where he was President and Founder, it was a pleasant surprise for most members to hear that Harry Edwards M.S.N.U. had accepted an invitation at the Conference of 1968 to become an Honorary Vice-President of the Union. The A.G.M. had to be re-convened because the accounts had not been presented in time. The accounts were late again the next year, 1969, and members were naturally perturbed at the amount of work the National Council was required to do. To try to solve this continuing dilemma a motion of devolvement was put for consideration. It was proposed to divide the country into four regions, each having their own council and taking over a proportion of the National Council's duties. This proposal was considered, but was rejected by the special committee designated to look again at these problems. Lily Shepherd, D Everitt, Dan Wright and Ray Taylor sat on this committee. H. Vigurs should have, but could not attend due to transport difficulties. When the special report was given it was explained that due to lack of finance, only one full meeting had been convened. That the Committee met at all was thanks to the London District Council who provided the funds. The meeting took place in February, 1970, for one brief week-end. In spite of this they had completed a tremendous amount of work. The solution, as they saw it, was to devolve much of the work presently done by the National Council to District level. They referred to the reports of 1965/66 which recommendations had not been implemented and also a change in the electoral system, which would mean each District Council would have representation on the Council. At that time there might have been more than one District represented by one Area representative. They highlighted the fact that come councillors had no specific duties, whereas others sat on more than one committee and that there was a sad lack of National policy. One very radical change recommended was that there should be a new smaller, active body called the 'National Executive Committee', responsible for the functioning of the Union in accordance with National Policy decided by the Council. The Council would appoint the N.E.C. annually to serve for a one year term of office. They saw no sense in transferring Headquarters to the Arthur Findlay College at Stansted, but did feel that a regular meeting place such as the A.F.C. gave a prestige which far outweighed any cost to the Union.

The report was surprisingly concise, given the breadth of their manifesto and the limitations in time and consultation between the members. It was left to the Council to consider, for many of the recommendations would require a change in the Articles and Bye-laws.

The subject of the A.F.C. was discussed at length. The finances needed to subsidise the work being done were frightening a lot of people. Findlay had given £29,000 for repairs. Apparently a great deal of money, but dry rot had forced the requirements far beyond this figure. Interest-free loans had been raised and money borrowed from the B.F.P. This was not popular in several areas because the amount borrowed meant that other Churches had to wait for their loans. Mr.L Wilson wanted to extend membership of the Board to non-Union Spiritualists, so that extra money could be made available. The membership voted strongly against this; they wanted the Hall to stay within the organisation of the Union in spite of its apparent liabilities. A suggestion was made that it should be the subject of a separate Trust. But Dr Winning explained that due to the conditions of the Deed of gift, it came under the conditions of the Memoranda of Association and it was not feasible to create a separate Trust for the college. Gordon Higginson proposed that many people might like to form a 'Friends of Stansted' and that this could defray some costs, as well as providing a pool of voluntary workers. This particular suggestion proved to be the most practical and indeed without its subsequent Society of Friends Stansted would be a poorer place.

Conference also heard that year that Council wanted to move the Union Headquarters from Manchester to Stansted. There had been doubts, but examination of the Trust Deed of the

Britten Memorial showed that it could be legally amended and therefore based in any part of the country. The Council recognised the members' objections to this move and realised that the Manchester District must have special consideration when the premises were sold, and Britten House transferred to Stansted. The money from the sale would not go into general funds, but would be invested and used for rent. Consideration was given to each District Council having their funds in a special trust, but this was vetoed by the members. Considering the perilous state of finance, clearly outlined by the incoming president Mr G Higginson, this showed a tremendous loyalty on the members' part. Percy Wilson stood up and stated that he and Mr Vigurs gave the Union less than two years lease of life unless matters improved. Bitter questions were asked as to why the B.F.P. had approved a loan of £64,000 to Stansted, and once again discussion took place on the benefits of selling the Hall.

1970 was a year when the members were informed quite clearly that they would have to decide whether or not they wanted to support their religion. In doing so they would have to put money as well as good wishes into the Union because, putting it bluntly, the Union was virtually bankrupt!

CHAPTER 9

ALL CARDS ON THE TABLE

Fighting Insolvency

When Gordon Higginson was elected President for the first time in 1970, he walked into a crisis situation. For a number of years the financial resources of the Union simply could not keep up with expenditure. A prime example of this was the fact that the Committee mandated to look into an alternative form of organisation to save money could not meet until the London District made funds available. There was no money in the kitty to pay their minimal expenses! Gordon, in his speech of acceptance, told the members the facts. If the Union was to survive, then the members were the only ones who could achieve this by giving their support and it would have to be generous support.

During the years of 1970/71 many meetings were held purely to raise money for the Union. Once again members were asked not only to donate money now, but to remember their religion when making their wills. Harry Edwards, Maurice Barbanell, Hannen Swaffer, they were but a few of those who rallied to the call for help sent out by Mr Higginson and the members of the Council; many made interest-free loans to help repay the costs of Stansted; even the Union of Spiritualist Mediums donated £50. The breach caused by the letters sent in 1959 asking the churches not to cooperate with this organisation and the Federation was healing in this time of trouble.

The Council of Spiritualists was created between the 'Big four', the S.N.U., S.A.G.B, G.W.S.L. and the U.S.M., to promote a better image of Spiritualism. A lot of work had to be undertaken that year, because due to changes in the law, changes had to be made in the Union's charitable registration. Also the way that ministers were appointed needed updating.

This was done, and a Ministers' Assessment Committee took charge of the task. The mood of change injected a feeling of re-generation into the organisation.

An offer of £100,000 had been made for Stansted Hall. But nothing definite had come of this offer and it was decided that there was no real point in discussing it. This did not prevent discussion taking place, but this was natural in view of the removal of the offices to Stansted and the general upheaval that this had caused. Gordon is now well-known for his preference that another should chair the .A.G.M. He offered an explanation for this when he asked D. Everitt, the Vice-President to chair. He wanted to listen and observe. He also felt that chairmen of the Standing Committees should accept the responsibility of answering the comments of members on the reports they had submitted. This has been the format since then and has recently been expanded so that the chairmen are available on the Friday evening to answer any questions that members want to ask, but do not feel warrant time taken during Conference. It has resulted in a greater awareness of personal responsibility within the Committees and participation with the members.

It was at Scarborough in 1974 that the Guild of Spiritualist Healers was declared a branch of the Union. The Guild had increased its membership. It now covered the country and wanted an independent identity, although it would still remain an integral part of the body of the Union.

We're In The Money! Well Almost...

In 1973 Mr. Higginson had been hopeful. He stated that within two years he anticipated, providing the members continued to pull together, overcoming the problems that threatened our existence. There were no plans to capitalise on any Union properties.

Indeed Mr. Higginson announced that the loan for Stansted had been repaid, and there were plans being made to open the Hall during the winter season, which would do a lot to offset the present expenditure over income.

Wilfred Potter, the treasurer, also had some good news, although there was a bitter side to it. He had discovered that income tax had not been recovered since 1965/66, resulting in a loss to the Union of £24,000. The most he could hope to recover was £1,400, but he was still looking into this. Even so, it meant that there would be a substantial increase in future income. The previous Headquarters in Manchester had been sold at auction and had realised £26,500, most of which had been invested as promised. Gordon actually resigned in March because the Council refused to support the plans made to pull the Union back from liquidation. He felt so strongly and was so inspired from Spirit, that a complete re-vamp was needed in the organisation, that he was prepared to step down completely rather than go against the inspiration. The Council, in view of this conviction, decided that they would give the scheme time and Gordon withdrew his resignation. Gordon always had faith in the Union and he saw Stansted as vitally important to the future. This is why he worked so very hard persuading members to support his vision.

It was declared during the meeting that there was a Trust controlling the London property in Doughty Street, although it appeared that it would not preclude the proceeds of any sale being used for work done at Stansted. Council's opinion was being referred to in order to clarify this point. One good sign that Spiritualists generally were thinking of the future was the opening of Brandon Lodge at Weston-Super-Mare, a home for elderly Spiritualists, workers or otherwise, who needed somewhere to live after retirement. This was done in conjunction with the Psychic Press who started a public appeal to pay for these premises.

A Revamp Long Overdue

The problem of finance was being dealt with on two fronts. One was income, the other expenditure. The main income of the Union came through subscriptions and capitation fees. These had been increased, but not sufficiently to allow for any extra expenditure. The problem was that with the increase in membership a greater burden of administration fell on the small office staff. Their wages were not high and more help was needed. At this time there was no chance of redressing the situation through the paid staff of the Union, but close attention was given to the expenses of committee work. No one on Union Committees was paid a salary, but travelling and board had to be paid for. Nothing must be wasted! Over the years several special committees had made reports on systems designed to improve the efficiency of the organised administration of Union affairs. They all agreed that simplification was required.

The 1969 report was the most comprehensive, in spite of the difficulty in meeting together. Mr Wilfred Watts had been appointed Secretary of a Drafting committee. After the 1973 conference he, together with J Calway and P Wilson, would be the non-council members qualified to deal with the drafting of the proposal to R Wilson and K Parish who would represent the Council. Wilfred Watts was asked to make a statement to Conference. The actual changes could not be made in 1974, because they required alteration to the bye-laws and the committee had not been able to submit these in time for notice to be given. The Scheme, which would be known as the 3 Tier System, was discussed at length. The problem was that the President was to appoint Chairmen of the Standing Committees, who together with the Vice- President and Treasurer would constitute the small National Executive Committee who would run the organisation. Many people, while accepting that Gordon Higginson travelled around the country and knew the capabilities of many members, felt future presidents might not be in the same position. This could lead to a president becoming a dictator by appointing 'Yes' men. Those who supported the scheme pointed out that the President and Vice-president are elected every year by all the members and could be thus taken out of office within twelve months. Legal advice had been given to the effect that the Council must be the policy- making body and must include the Officers of the Union as well as the representatives of the various areas and branches. The discussion ended, at least officially, and instructions were given to amend the articles to incorporate the changes required. But the discussion continued through the year; Spiritualists no longer sent such long letters of argument and debate about matters of policy to the journals, but this was different. Not only members but the editors of various journals took up deliberation, some in vitriolic fashion. They referred to past complaints made about the Union and various personel within the structure, particularly the President, Gordon Higginson. At times these comments became quite vicious. Not even the editor of the 'Psychic News' escaped attack for his comments on the situation. Not that he fully supported the change, but he did maintain a reasonable impartiality. Never-the-less, the majority of members recognised the necessity for a greater degree of specialisation. The right person for the right job! The work done for the Union far outweighed any past problems, which had been properly dealt with anyway!

CHAPTER 10

RADICAL CHANGES

That which stagnates, dies!

The discussion continued through the year of 1975, and into the next A.G.M.The new form of organisation was radical. That it was also sensible and more economical went by the board in many people's opinion. For them it seemed as if the hierarchy were striking at the very roots of their democratic freedom. Fortunately there were many who thought the matter through and realised that the President could be deposed quite easily if an oligarchal clique seemed to be forming. It was W. Tyler of Gloucester who moved the motion to adopt the Three Tier System. After all the discussion of the previous year, this could have been a formality. But still members wanted to express their feelings. The Lyceum representation had been two and now would only be one on Council. Dr. Hopkins also worried that the D.C. representatives would be unable to express a national viewpoint. In the end Mr. Tyler reminded Conference of a statement made by Percy Wilson, that he had received numerous messages from our pioneers that the Union must be rebuilt from rock bottom.

The motion was put to the members and carried with the required three-quarter majority. In future the National Executive Committee would administer the affairs of the Union, the Council would formulate policy and the District Councils and the Branches would have their prescribed duties, which would include electing their representative to Council. It was hoped that having a much smaller group to direct the affairs of the Union would reduce expenditure. By virtue of having the chairmen of the Standing Committees appointed for ability, it was hoped to increase efficiency. A certain element of democracy

72

was retained in that nominations for the positions would be sent in by post from members. This would serve another purpose: if quite a few nominations were received for a person whose ability was not known to the President or Vice-President then enquiries could be made and if suitable the nominee might be invited on to a Committee where they could be useful.

The Division of London

In December 1974 a meeting of members of the London District had been called to discuss the intention of the Council to divide the District in two. The members did not want this; the London District was the first to apply to the Union to be known by this title, and they did not want to be changed. It was considered whether a Commission of Enquiry should be constituted in reference to the Council's plans to take over Doughty Street and a motion was put at Conference asking for a full explanation as to why the Council had gone against the members' express disapproval. The newly formed W.L.D.C. had voted against supporting this motion as they considered it would cause bad feeling between East and West London. The Council had by then taken legal advice that their headquarters in Doughty St. had a separate Trust and the London District had taken the first steps to sell the property. This forestalled a lot of argument; although the different Districts had several times supported the Union by voting against having their monies put into separate Trusts, there were those who were very suspicious of the proposed take-over of Doughty St. This was very much rumour. But rumours can activate fears far more efficiently than facts.

There was still a lot of opposition to the new Three Tier system. Mr Hopkins had tried, at the 1976 conference to have this changed. Fortunately enough people felt that this was not giving the system time to be tried. The policy of the Union was to try for greater efficiency. Even the assessment of Ministers was under review. By 1977 the possibility of bridging the gap between the Lyceum and Union Educational Courses was considered, and the Guild of Spiritualist Healers felt that a separate Trust was warranted. But it was decided that this was not so,

73

neither would the individual D.C.'s funds or Stansted Hall be regarded as separate from the Union assets.

A scheme was put to the members which would mean that the huge outstanding debt on Stansted would be repaid. It meant moving funds from several sources, but the advice of the solicitors and accountants had been sought and they had agreed. Mr Higginson pointed out that this would mean that Stansted could now go forward to fulfil its rightful purpose. He had always seen the possibilities of a centre for training which would have international standing. The Hall was not perfect for a college, but it was adequate. It was a status symbol and it was ours!

'If you can face both triumph and disaster..'

1978 was a particularly difficult year for the Union. First, our President Mr Higginson had been accused of fraud. Accused on the flimsiest of evidence, indeed, not even evidence but suspicion.This accusation was not made directly to Gordon, but made via the media. Maurice Barbanell editor of the 'Psychic News' also received a letter and was the one who had to tell Gordon about the sorry affair. The national press had a field day and this in turn led to other unpleasant incidents. Twice the police were informed that a bomb had been planted at Gordon's home; once even at his Church. His accuser would not make a statement to the special committee set up to investigate the affair and solicitors had to be employed. Mr Higginson had offered to resign and stated this in his address to Conference. Even that weekend, further rumours which had no truthful foundation whatsoever, about the church in question had been reported nationally. The members in Conference confirmed their support for their President. But the stress of such upset greatly affected his health.

That was not the end of the year's troubles. In November, an article appeared in a Spiritualist journal making serious allegations about the Union, its officers and Stansted. An apology and retraction of the libel was demanded but was not received. There was little moral choice. Legal proceedings were instituted, and once again the Union prepared to defend its name. The jury found the article to be defamatory; costs and damages were awarded; these were not paid! The instigator of this nasty piece of mischief-making, the writer, did not even trouble to appear in court. No one can really assess the feeling of hurt and sense of outrage that such matters engender; even when the Union's officials and all who were involved were exonerated a feeling of triumph was the last emotion experienced. In Gordon's words: 'I felt a great sadness, a deep weariness of Spirit that men who call themselves brother Spiritualists could inflict so much damage on our organisation'. There are no winners of such conflict. All loyal members felt the hurt of those who had been pilloried and showed clearly their continued loyalty and trust.

Another change in title-'Limited' deleted!
Business could not be suspended just because of difficulty. In 1979 Mrs Hudson, who has since accepted the position of Hon. Vice-President of the S.N.U., stated she had been looking into methods to simplify the administrative work which added to the expense of running the Union. One proposal was that we should separate the incorporated body, leaving the religious body as the holding company and not effected by the Companies Act. Some were for, others against. Nothing new in Spiritualism, for they are a body of individuals usually with strong views on most things. The N.E.C. were asked to look at this scheme. As the Capital debt on Stansted had been extinguished, the N.E.C. took great pleasure in proposing that all loans outstanding should be paid, and that any funds remaining in the President's Appeal should be transferred to the S.N.U. ArthurFindlay College Foundation Fund which was set up in such a way that only the interest could be used. Although the motion to change yet again the basic structure or make-up of the Union was defeated that year,many people really disliked the word 'Limited' which was part of the official title. Advice was sought and had been received from the Companies Registrar; alterations were made to the Memorandum and Articles, were approved by the members and 'Limited' was dropped from our name.

Once again the subject of whether Ministers should have to be Diploma Holders was raised at Conference. Many people considered that the individual's spiritual quality and work done should be sufficient qualification. The opposing factions declared that the Minister's Award, being the highest the Union offered, must have integrity. Ministers must know about their religious organisation so that they could not only adhere to its legal requirements, but be able to advise others and speak publicly on the subject. The appointing of Ministers had been brought in for a number of reasons, not least of which was the fact that it gave a basis of respectability and permanence to our movement. People who did not understand the religious side of Spiritualism, but only knew about communication, recognised the title as belonging solely to religion. We will hopefully one day be regarded as a religion on a par with other great world religions. Those whom we regard as our Ministers must be able to deal on equal terms with people who have received long and arduous training in their chosen religion. It was therefore vital that our Ministers too should have at least some rudimentary training. The work required to achieve this must be of equal importance to the spirituality displayed by the potential Ministers; they would be dealing with practical issues as well as moral dilemmas. The majority of members agreed with this concept and the matter was decided.

Members, aware of the change of status of the council, now a policy-making but not directive body, changed control of the Building Fund Pool to its members. From now on there would be postal ballots for elections, at least as soon as the Trust Deed was amended. This change actually took place in 1981 when the mandated document was agreed at Conference. At that time, individual members were not acceptable to the B.F.P.Scheme and so only the Class A delegates voted.

A Welcome Injection of Capital

A great deal of concern was expressed because so much time was taken up at Conference for business This meant that little time was given to discussing policy. The problem was, of course, that many matters were brought up in the meeting that could have been resolved in other ways. There was also very little future policy being formulated at that time. True, certain matters had been resolved which allowed future plans to be made, but these were limited within groups, the B.F.P. and A.F.C. being two. It was perhaps a culmination of the support so recently given by members when the President of Cambridge Spiritualist Church, Mr R G Olsson stood to announce that his members had agreed to donate £5,000 to assist with the upkeep of Britten House at Stansted. Only the interest was to be used and so this sum would give a regular income. They also agreed to invest £15000, and would give all the interest of this to the Trust Property Committee to help other churches. A wonderful and generous gesture which was very welcome. Another easing of the financial burden of the Union came with the sale of Doughty Street in London. The money was to be put in Trust but would be used to underwrite the expenses of both London District Councils as well as helping other District Councils in certain ways. As usual, not everyone agreed to this plan, and as it was not the jurisdiction of the Union only discussion and not voting took place.

Periodically through the history of the Union the problem of Christian Spiritualism was raised. It was not a problem to the Union that it existed, although the fact that Spiritualism had split into two camps effectively weakened the whole of the movement. No, it was the gradual infiltration of this practice and teachings into Union churches that caused the main concern.There was quite a lot of discussion in the Union in the early 1980's, debating this problem. Each time the question of true Spiritualism was addressed, a majority of members put National Spiritualism first. But there was a hard core who advocated tolerance. For this reason few directives had been given in reference to the principles of this controversial subject and a few D.C.'s found that they had serious problems with some of their churches. This was a minority but resulted in disharmony.

The Three Tier System was still viewed with suspicion by some. The fear of oligarchy had been expressed right from the start of organisation and was at the root of repeated attempts to get the system changed again.

The changes in the education system to bring it more into line with conventional examination study courses was not fully understood, or always appreciated where it was understood. It was however generally agreed that the standards of workers needed to be improved, even if the methods of achieving this could not be agreed. Stansted Hall was often a point of discussion, even argument. It was the home of the Arthur Findlay College, which was intended to be the educational establishment of the Union. Unfortunately it had to become financially viable and could not at that time do so by only promoting Union practices. The main debt had been paid, but the upkeep was horrendous. The possibilities of the nearby airport being expanded meant that the value of the Hall had increased: those who supported the principle of having a prestigious college and established Head Office feared this might tempt a future sale, thus leaving the Union with only monetary gain. There were many who saw the Hall in the past light of a drain on the resources of the Union, limited in its location, being South rather than central, and felt that it would be sensible to find alternative premises better designed to function as a College. In the end a compromise was reached. A motion was put desiring future generations to rehouse the A.F.C. if at any time Stansted Hall should be sold. Legally present members could not bind future members to do this, but could put it on record that they wanted the work of the College to be safeguarded, no matter what.

CHAPTER 11

THE UNION MOVES AHEAD

A Lack of Communication-In Spiritualism?

People felt very strongly that there was a lack of communication between the three tiers and the members. Several in-house publications had been started and had not been supported. The feeling about lack of communication was right, and it was far more widespread than most would admit. Many church members, even officials, did not truly know what the S.N.U. was or what it stood for. Many considered that they were paying capitation fees for nothing. Few recognised the benefits of affiliation to the Union. Very little positive publicity had been generated to inform members of the benefits of affiliation. The older members recognised what a difference legal acceptance made to their activities, but those just coming in did not!. They had not known the years when a medium could be prosecuted, and did not even think about freedom of worship. It was there; a right which was taken for granted! Even if some one mentioned: 'The old days of persecution' few went on to explain that without the strength of National Organisation and the determination of the Union their present 'rights' would not exist. This was a matter that should be rectified. But at that time, no-one was given the responsibility.

A great deal of financial pressure had been eased in November 1981 when the Charity Commissioners passed their sealed order agreeing the sale of Doughty Street. The monies from this would be invested in the London Headquarters Fund, a subsidiary charity of the S.N.U.,regulated by the scheme of the Charity Commissioners of the 6th April, 1981. The L.H.F. would underwrite the expenses of the two London District Councils; other Districts would be able to apply for certain activities to be paid for and for some equipment to be supplied. In return, the London Districts would transfer most of their funds to the L.H.F. and would waive their right to the proportion of capitation fees normally transferred from the Union. This transfer meant that District Councils had an assured income; the London Districts would now rely on the L.H.F. There would be six Trustees, three appointed from each D.C. The L.H.F. promised to offset the Union overdraft for three years and future financing of the two London Districts. Further help was given when the L.H.F. bought Redwoods, a small house in the grounds of Stansted Hall, from the Union and refurbished it to be used as the Union H.Q. office. This released the rooms of Britten House, again, in the grounds of Stansted, to be used for committee members needing accommodation or, when not needed, the overflow of guests at the Hall. Rent was paid to the Britten Memorial Trust, the Union had Offices for a peppercorn rent and the Union had first refusal if ever the L.H.F. decided to re-sell Redwoods.

Mundane But Necessary

The excitement of this L.H.F. occupied Conference for several years until it was pointed out what the Charity Commissioners had elected to do and that the Fund was not required to report to the members; it was autonomous in nature and the Trustees were answerable only to the Charity Commissioners.

By 1984 a report had been compiled in favour of the three tier system. Eric Hatton, the Vice-President had sent out hundreds of forms so that the committee could get a national feedback. Some members still wanted change in the system and a motion proposing the introduction of a postal ballot for Special Resolutions. Often at Conference only about ten percent of members attended, leaving the majority non-participating in the Union business. The main argument against this suggestion was that there would then be no sense in discussing motions, as only those present would be in a position to hear the pros and cons, and perhaps change their minds. This could lead to lack of interest in attending. Churches would not pay for representation if what was said was going to make little difference to the eventual result. This was a valid argument and carried the day. Members felt that we should be looking for greater involvement at Conference, not less.

Since the Healing Guild has been made a Branch, there had been some misunderstandings about their authority in the Healing Courses and their position in the churches. This was discussed, argued at length and it was clarified that the churches did not want and would not accept the Guild's jurisdiction in what were their own affairs and that any course work, other than the Lyceum was done in the name of the Union; not a Branch. The Healing Diploma had been in existence since the early 1950's and the Healing Committee well before that date. This extensive discussion cleared up not only misunderstandings but some tensions which had built because of a lack of communication.

During 1984/85 the first Ministers' Conferences were held. Very little positive results come from these, but it had given the opportunity for ministers to meet together to discuss their responsibilities and duties. One point of recommendation raised considerable controversial debate; the adoption of our academic gown to be worn on official occasions! There was very little general support for this move: it was seen as a move towards orthodoxy, and although supported by both N.E.C. and Council, was eventually thrown out by members in General Meeting.

Although not a part of the Union, it would be wrong not to mention the existence of the Confederation of Healing Organisations. The Union was one of the founding members of this organisation, which was doing valuable work in bringing together various healing organisations. The Treasurer of the Union, Mr. Wilfred Watts, was also the Treasurer of the C.H.O. They had negotiated with the hierarchy of the orthodox medical profession. Several research projects were in hand and a certain degree of co-operation had been achieved with doctors and hospitals. An important offshoot of this was the instigation of an insurance scheme which was acceptable to the medical profession and beneficial to all participating healers. An appeal was being launched to raise £500,000 for initial research, that orthodoxy insisted upon before any conclusions about the benefit of spiritual healing could be declared.

It was the Guild Code of Ethics which had been used as the basis of the accepted C.H.O. Code of Conduct. The Guild was expanding and wanted to expand further. They asked in 1985 for members to work towards the principle that all healers in S.N.U. churches should become Guild members. Whereas the principle of this was recognised, after all the Union Healing Committee had started the Guild in the first place, the concept caused controversy in the churches. There the president was responsible together with the healing leader and they decided who should be a qualified church healer. Some of these chose to belong to the Guild and/or other healing organisations. They did not want to be told which one they should join.

After a period of comparative calm, the subject of true National Spiritualism once again came to the fore. A number of churches were being affected by the determined efforts of a new Christian Spiritualist organisation; others, possibly encouraged by this, had declared a dual loyalty to the G.W.S.L. and the S.N.U. With a few the latter was considered the lesser loyalty and these made moves towards dis-affiliation. This of course was their democratic right and could be achieved through the constitution of the Union rules. What could not be done was to transfer the Trust Deed. That part referred not to members who had the right to decide in favour of dis-affiliation, but the Trust involved the building. If this had been placed in trust by the founding members for a specific purpose i.e. National Spiritualism, then it could not just be altered. Some churches felt that as the monies loaned to either start or substantially improve their premises had been repaid then they should be free to take back their deeds and go their own way, following which path they chose. Members in meeting in 1985 discussed the implications of Christian symbols and practices being used in many churches. New churches had to agree not to use these, but those already in affiliation had rights of tradition. The majority felt that there should be guide-lines compiled and sent to churches.

The London Headquarters Fund Buys 'The Two Worlds'

No, not here and beyond, but the journal started by Emma Hardinge-Britten. A publication always closely linked with the Union, its editors always having held position within the Council. One request the Fund had received was that there should be a church magazine. In 1981 the Trustees decided to use their resources to start publishing a magazine called 'Here and There'. Published in 1982 initially for the London area it has been expanded to cover much of the country. . Before this could be done a Company, The Headquarters Publishing Company, had to be formed. This Company started to publish Spiritualist literature and books.The L.H.F., since its inception in 1980 had used its considerable resources many times on behalf of the Union and so when the President,Gordon Higginson, made a direct request that the L.H.F. should purchase the rights of title of the 'Two Worlds' from the Psychic Press there was a subsidiary Company available to take up this challenge. The Union was of course trustee, but the journal was, as it always had been,independent. At first it was edited by Kay Hunter, but then Ray Taylor took over. Working in a voluntary capacity, he persuaded more and more National Spiritualists to contribute to the contents and struggled to make ends meet. Conference after conference had discussed the need to have some publication that was their own. Here was an opportunity; they could make the 'Two Worlds' their own in all but ownership. For many years, while owned by Psychic Press and other shareholders, the 'Two Worlds' had given two pages a month to reporting SNU news. Ray Taylor, a member of the N.E.C., was willing to publish any articles or news sent to him either in the 'Two Worlds' or in its sister magazine, 'Here and There'. All he asked was the support of members so that the publications should not be a drain on the London Headquarters Fund. This support was given only in part. Some argued that it was not owned by the S.N.U. and did not publish news and views exclusive to Union philosophy. That the editor was wholly loyal to the Union, indeed was largely responsible for many successful financial investments made to its benefit, that the board of Directors consisted of Union personnel two of whom were officers, the

President, Gordon Higginson and the Treasurer, Wilfred Watts, did not make any difference to their dissension, voiced at first quite frequently. Those most frequently heard were those least willing to contribute articles of Union interest so that the magazine truly reflected Union views.

Keeping The Roof On

Gradually the Union was pulling together. Ideas were muted to sort out the library system; not only to categorise but possibly to microfilm. The cost was considered prohibitive for the latter plan, but it was put aside for when the money would be available. Mr Taylor highlighted most graphically not only at Conference, but in print, the need for extensive review of church upkeep. Many church committees did not have the knowledge necessary to spot potential danger areas. Often the warden or trustee was equally ignorant. This had resulted in some churches falling virtually into decay and being faced with crippling repair bills. A campaign was started in 1986 to popularise the five year surveys. Ray Taylor pointed out that there just was not enough money to give all the help that was needed. Only a few out of over three hundred churches in trust had bothered to give money to the Trust Property Committee and in this Cambridge led the way. He appealed to all churches who were able to give cash assistance to their fellow churches in need to do so; too many churches had a parochial attitude and did not truly feel themselves as part of a larger organisation. This was of course partly the fault of the organisation. In order to lend money at a lower rate of interest, the Building Fund Pool had to offer less interest than outside sources. They did their best to keep the lending rate low and the investment return high, but there would always be a differential. New methods were devised; individual investments were allowed for the first time in 1988. This encouraged members to use the Pool as a savings account, in similar fashion to a Building Society. They would sacrifice very little, about one percent, one pound in a hundred; their help would mean so much! Many members responded to this and the Pool attracts new investors every year.

To The End Of The Century And Further Change

No-one wanted indoctrination, but no move was made to ensure that members fully understood what the Union was or what it stood for before they were accepted into full membership. This basic flaw could only be fully resolved by the churches and their committees. Far more publicity was needed, and this needed to be backed by up-to-date literature. During 1985/6 a series of Publicity meetings had been organised. They were not given the support needed in every District to ensure complete success. Many Districts felt that there had been too little consultation and inadequate forethought. A rally had been organised in Hyde Park, London, but due to problems with the authorities, who had allocated a rather secluded spot where there were few passers-by, and lack of publicity the meeting had been much smaller than anticipated. It was however friendly. Gordon hoped to plan something along the lines of a March in the Centenary year, 1990. The sale of Redwoods was completed, and the capital safely invested, which meant that the Union had a substantial sum of money from the interest to help with ever-rising costs of organisation.

Due to the mandates passed at recent A.G.M.'s on policy put forward by the Council, (representing every D.C., Branch and Member of the Union), it was recognised that the Rule Book would need extensive revision. This was done by the Conference in 1987, although there were printing problems, so the books were not available till later. All churches were advised that these would supersede any Rules in existence. This meant that any deviation would have to be submitted to the NEC and approved. The main and controversial change was that no S.N.U.Church could continue with dual affiliation with another religion, nor could any person holding any position within a body holding principles deemed to be incompatible with the seven Principles hold Office within the S.N.U. This was a fairly obvious move and long overdue.The mandate of members to the Executive in 1983, that from that time all newly affiliated churches would have signed a pledge not to display the symbols and trappings of other religions, showed the desire of the ma-

85

1 **Emma Hardinge Britten.** Founder and Editor of "Two Worlds", Emma travelled the world promoting the philosophy of Spiritualism. She ended her life in Britain, the country of her birth, having helped to promote the National Federation of Spiritualist Churches which later expanded and changed its name to the Spiritualists' National Union (of churches).

2 **George Berry** (1920 - 1922). George had the difficult task of steering through the new Memorandum and Articles of Association. He was also Secretary of the Union for some time.

3 **Jessie Greenwood** (1923 - 1925). Jessie was the President of the SLU as well as being the only woman President the Union has elected.

4 **Ernest Keeling** (1928 - 1930). A man of humour and charm, he helped prepare the way for the Parliamentary Bill to be presented to the House of Commons.

5 **J.B. McIndoe** (1930 - 1938). A modest man, during his term of office the draft Bill was presented to Parliament and a new Bill was prepared. He instigated the Freedom Fund in 1943.

6 **Frank Blake** (1938 - 1941). A strong, quiet man, his responsibilities were increased by the outbreak of war.

7 **John Stewart** (1941 - 1943). Helped to promote the short-lived Youth Movement and worked hard to bring about harmony between the SLU and the Union.

8 **Harold Vigurs** (1943 - 1948). He was an important civil servant who brought his expertise to bear within the Union, particularly during the problems of Helen Duncan's trial. Well known for his exposition of the Seven Principles.

9 **W.L. Haig** (1948 - 1950). A man of high principles and dedication. During his term of office the SLU amalgamated with the Union. The Witchcraft Act of 1735 was repealed and section 4 of the Vagrancy Act, 1824, amended.

10 **Percy Wilson** (1952 - 1953). Brought many new churches into Trust with the Union. A prosaic man, he did not see the role of leadership within the Union as spiritual but as administrative.

11 **Harry Dawson** (1953 - 1958). He was one of the Presidents to negotiate the acceptance of Stansted Hall on behalf of the Union. He was also pleased to accept shares in Psychic Press from Maurice Barbanell.

12 **Charles Quastel** (1965 - 1968). Famous for his desire to unite all Spiritualist organisations under one banner - the Union!

13 **Dr. J. Winning** (1965 - 1968). Permitted televising to take place at Stansted Hall for the first time and supported the attempts to have greater representation of Districts.

14 **J. Arthur Findlay** MBE JP (1883 - 1964). Born in Glasgow, Mr. Findlay made his fortune in business, was given the Freedom of the City in 1920 and converted to Spiritualism soon after. The first of his many books on the subject, "On the Edge of the Etheric", was published in 1931. He addressed many large meetings in England and Europe and took a prominent part in the Church of Scotland's enquiry into Spiritualism in 1920. He willed his family home, Stansted Hall, to be used as a college for psychic studies. He was honorary President of the Union.

15   **Stansted Hall**. Bequeathed to the SNU by Sir Arthur Findlay, this magnificent house set in spacious grounds has retained its atmosphere of peace and dignity while being brought up to date as a college open to the public. Visitors come regularly from all over the world to take part in the weekly courses of spiritual and psychic learning.

16 **Sir Arthur Conan Doyle.** Honorary President of the International
Spiritual Congress, President of the London Spiritual Alliance and
Hon. President in Spirit of the Spiritualists' National Union. Known
as the "St. Paul of Spiritualism", from 1916 he and his wife devoted
themselves to the promotion of Spiritualism.

17 **Estelle Roberts**, one of the best known British mediums ever. Demonstrated on more than one occasion at the Albert Hall. Medium of Red Cloud.

18 **Helen Duncan**, a superb materialisation medium. She stood trial at the Old Bailey under the infamous Witchcraft Act.

19 **Bertha Harris**, as a young medium, 'Battling Bertha', she appeared on platform with Sir Arthur Conan Doyle.

20 **Eileen Garrett** was well known in Britain and became one of the best known mediums in America.

21 **William Redmund** MSNU, has been called a human telephone. He has dedicated his life to propagating the teachings and philosophy of National Spiritualism. William has worked with most of the great names of the past.

22 **Harry Edwards** MSNU. One of the finest healing mediums of this century and Founder of the NSFH. Harry was not only a Minister and supporter of the SNU but was also an Honorary Vice-President.

23 **Maurice Barbanell** MSNU. Nicknamed "Mr. Spiritualism" or "Barbie" he spent over 60 years as a spectator and participator in the ringside of Spiritualism. Founder of "Psychic News" and medium of one of the world's best-known and loved guides, Silver Birch. Benefactor and Minister of the SNU.

24 **Alfred Kitson.** Known as the "Father of the British Lyceum Movement". Co-compiler and author of the Lyceum Manual.

25 **Hannen Swaffer**. Known as the "Pope of Fleet Street". Helped to bring a respect for Spiritualism within the popular press. He is best remembered as the instigator and host of the circle through which Silver Birch communicated for so many years.

26 **Gordon Higginson** MSNU. A life-long Spiritualist, his name is synonymous with the Spiritualists' National Union. Elected President every year since 1970, Gordon has devoted his life to the propogation of National Spiritualism in Britain. One of the first British mediums to demonstrate in Europe, he is the Principle of Stansted Hall and President of his own church at Longton.

jority of members to assume their own identity and declare it to the world!

It had been realised for some time that a firm stand would have to be made if the basic philosophy of National Spiritualism was to be perpetuated. Christian Spiritualist Ministers were attending, sometimes working in our churches wearing the traditional garb of the orthodox Christian Church which they had adopted as their own. Mr Bendall, a former President of the G.W.C.S.L., had decried this custom in the G.W. journal in 1953, but it was obviously now acceptable. Some mediums who were not even accepted as ministers were going around with clerical collars and big crosses. Complaints had been made, but now directive was needed. The Union had tried to arrange discussions with the G.W. to come to agreement. At least ten churches were being run by declared Christians on Christian lines. A small minority, but too many for a religion which was open, because of its declared freedom of philosophy, to people of all other religious. The signing of the Seven Principles should have protected the possibility of this eventuality, but many of the people concerned used our traditional tolerance against us. They stated that their 'liberty of interpretation' gave them the freedom to include a belief in Christianity while following Spiritualism. Gordon Higginson put the feeling of the majority of members into a few words at Conference: "I have nothing against Christian Spiritualism, but if the church was National Spiritualist then it must remain National Spiritualist. If they did not want this then they should find their own buildings and not pinch ours!"

The subject of Liberty of Interpretation caused even more dissent. This phrase had been part of our tradition from around 1902. It was not part of the Memorandum or the Articles of Association, but had been viewed with pride by generations. No- one had considered that it would be used in such a way as to distort the essence of our Principles. Because of this, a member of Council queried the legal validity of the phrase. Legal advice was sought and the Union was advised that the phrase had no meaning or validity in the context of a legal framework. It was with some regret that it was withdrawn from general usage. But the Union pointed out that 'Personal Responsibility' covered each individual's right to think for his or herself, whereas the Churches did have to stay within the cover of the Memorandum and Articles without personal interpretation.

Even membership was considered that year of 1988. Class B membership was brought into line with the churches, in as much as a probationary period of twelve months maximum would be required.

1989 was a year of consolidation and effort. A new formula was tried at Conference to try to speed up the business procedure. The various members of the Standing Committees made themselves available on the Friday evening to answer any questions that could be dealt with outside the main meeting. This had limited success; many members did not realise that they could go in without prior notice; some did not know where the room was! In other words, it had not yet become an established procedure. It was agreed that the idea was good and should become a regular feature of Conference. Again, the consultative conference suffered in the same way on the Sunday afternoon. Instead of discussing future policy, the meeting resulted in discussion of what had been done. A new type of award was announced, the first for many years. It had become obvious that there was a need for more people capable of officiating at funerals, naming services and marriages, but not necessarily qualified to become Ministers. The position of Officiant covered these requirements. In slightly different vein but following the same theme; the position of approved Celebrant was established to cover the particular requirements of Scottish law. The bye-laws were amended to comply with legal requirements.

A great deal of time was given to the arrangements in hand for the following year's centenary celebrations. The N.E.C., in response to the members wishes voiced at the previous A.G.M., had created a new Standing Committee: Publicity and Public Relations. It had not been financially possible to appoint a paid public relations officer, as had been wanted, but Mrs. Jean Bassett, the Chairman, would do her best in that capacity. The celebrations were to start with a Grand Publicity Meeting arranged at Wembley in London and would continue through every District of the Union. A special fund had been started by Mr. Higginson. This would subsidise any District that could not pay its way and would be for use within various areas of publicity. It was hoped that this would include the further training of mediums capable of taking future publicity meetings. The members greeted these plans of the N.E.C. with enthusiasm. The concept of greater professionalism was in line with the changes that had taken place over the past few years and would hopefully take Spiritualism into the twenty- first century with a crisper image.

One problem that still had not been dealt with was that of the Christian influx of S.N.U. churches. If, as was visualised, we were going to be able to present Spiritualism outside the Churches to people who were not committed, then this subject required urgent attention. For many years the Union had been corresponding with the G.W. on the issue of basic identity. The most recent correspondence started in 1984 when the G.W. announced the establishment of a Ministry and wrote to the Union suggesting a meeting. The Union agreed and in December that year the subject of the compatibility or otherwise of the Seven Principles with the G.W. Declaration of Belief, the problems of dual membership and the presence of Christian trappings in S.N.U. churches was discussed. At a further meeting it was decided that the S.N.U. Principles and the G.W. Pledge were not compatible. Churches in Trust should relinquish membership with the G.W., whilst others should make their own choice, as should members of those holding awards of either organisation. This was of course a preliminary statement of agreement. A report and joint statement was to be prepared and published. However, in October 1985 Mrs Beattie Scott wrote and stated that the Greater World were willing to talk, but a joint statement would be inappropriate. This, after so long, was a bitter blow to the Union. The lapse in time could not be blamed on anyone. The G.W. had pressing internal affairs to see to and Mrs Scott had not long joined them; she had felt, quite correctly, that she needed to know more of the subject before writing. The Union did respond, asking the G.W. to reconsider the last meeting. But no positive response came until late the next year, when once again a meeting was planned although no date agreed.

In the meantime the position within a few S.N.U. churches deteriorated. Quite a lot of members felt that the Union were being dogmatic and that all should be free to follow their own instincts. Half the problem was a lack of positive identity. Many churches had officials who knew very little about the Union, did not know what benefits they accrued from affiliation and resented the affiliation fees, feeling that the Union only ever took and gave nothing in return. Quite a number of members did not know that the Union had never been Christian-orientated and no one had ever explained to them why not. Many Churches displayed Christian symbols and pictures and recited the 'Lord's Prayer'. They neither recognised nor felt any real difference from the church of their childhood. When in February 1987 the NEC, having been mandated at previous A.G.M.'s, finally approved new Rules which would make the position of the Union much clearer to these members and to any new member, there was uproar. Even more so than when the Conditions for Affiliation were amended to ensure that every new church would sign a promise not to use the trappings of other religions. That engendered the usual cry of bigotry and dogmatism. Many churches felt threatened, because they read it that the ruling would apply to all affiliated churches instead of only new churches coming into affiliation. Most who objected, particularly in the South, could not recognise that Christian symbols were not acceptable to non-Christians and were liable to create, through association, a Christian identity in the minds of those who came into their churches. When at the end of 1987 the new diaries were printed with the magic phrase, 'Liberty of Interpretation' missing, there was even greater furore, indignation and letters to the press. For a while it seemed as if no-one supported the policies of the Union. Some District Council Executives had a rough ride; they were the third tier and more closely in contact with members' feelings of outrage. The tackling of this problem was long overdue; if it had been done when it was first recognised as a problem then possibly such extreme measures might not have been needed. The Union had taken legal advice on the

'Liberty of Interpretation' phrase and had presented this as a statement at the Conference in 1988. It was seen by Council as being 'ultra vires', void from the beginning, as not being contained within the Memorandum, it should not appear in the Articles or any other Official document. Members did not like this at all. They asked, quite reasonably, why allow something to go on so long if it is not legal? The answer was, of course, that until certain groups started to use the phrase to interpolate a Christian bias to the S.N.U philosophy, no one had reason to investigate the matter. To permit a mistake to continue just because it had been made for years was not a good policy and the N.E.C. had decided to act now rather than leave it for another Committee to deal with. The Union was tired of the long term, intermittent wrangling that took place between the Christian Spiritualist and the National Spiritualist. Only by firmly establishing boundaries of identity could this position be rectified. Once that had been achieved and publicised, then perhaps all the arguments would cease and each would get on with their own work in their own way.

By the time the 1990's dawned, it was obvious to the Executive that the Union really was pulling together. With great enthusiasm and hard work each District had organised celebrations,. a number in partnership with the Lyceum movement who were of course celebrating their own Centenary. Great effort was being made to improve the communication between N.E.C., Council and members. Some approaches had been made by the National Media. Naturally these had to be taken carefully. Much damage had been done in the past when they had taken events and words out of context, more particularly when the Union and genuine Spiritualism had been confused with psychics and fortune-telling. It is a sad reflection that one hundred years after our start as a national body of Spiritualists, we have not yet projected our identity as a genuine religion with a philosophy that could change the ways of the world. The pioneers of the past built what we have today. It is up to us, the members of today to work for the future. We can do it, I have no doubts:

CHAPTER 12

THE ORGANISATION OF THE UNION

The District Councils

District Councils are basically the life blood of the Union.

They are the churches and the Class B members of an area of the country and are termed a Branch of the Union. Not in quite the same way that the Lyceum and the Healing Guild are Branches, but with the same rights of representation: a member on the Council and a delegate with voting rights at the A.G.M.

It is through the nominations of the Class B members and the churches that the chair-persons of the Standing Committees have the right to be appointed and the President and the Vice-president are elected. If these nominations are not received, then no matter how suitable an individual might be, or no matter how much they are wanted as chair-persons, they do not qualify and cannot be chosen.

District Councils were formed where there were enough churches to warrant this. In 1904 there were three: N.E.Lancs, Manchester, S.E.Lancs., and negotiations were going on with Nottingham. It was first suggested at the A.G.M. of 1906, at Holborn Library, that this should be extended to the whole country. John Adams, during his Presidential Address, informed everyone that the subject would be open for discussion. But in anticipation, the Union of London Spiritualists had petitioned the National Executive Council that, "They may become the London District Executive of the Spiritualist National Union."

It was some years before the whole of the country was covered and divided into Districts. In 1911 the 'Potteries' completed the National Grid. This method of internal government is valuable to the national organisation, as it keeps a continuation of loyalty to people who are known and trusted. The

91

churches, societies and individual members within each District are responsible for the election of their own officers and members of their District Executive. These are often the people who will move on to national committees. In this way everyone has a say, to some extent, in what is going on in the Union.

Each affiliated church, according to the number of full members, has a Class A representative who will reflect the views of the members of the church. A lot of churches do not emphasise the fact that in their General Meeting the members should vote on any matter that is to be brought up at District level. If their representative is going to Conference, then they will have a vote; and they can vote according to how the church feels, which may vie with the consensus of the whole District because they represent a number of people, who obviously pay more for the upkeep of the Union than does one Class B. Then they are entitled to more voting strength (5 votes) at both District and National level. A lot of people do not realise that as members of affiliated churches they do have a say in the running of the Union by virtue of their vote.

There have been arguments in the past that people who join as Church members should automatically become subscribing members of the Union. Against this concept, is the fact that many people join Churches without necessarily thinking along Union lines. Sometimes they are lonely, sometimes they just like the way the Church is run or the activities arranged. Perhaps they ought to; after all, if one joins the C. of E. Church, one automatically becomes a member of the Church of England; again, a Union Member must desire to really support Union philosophy and activity. Not always the same thing as Church Membership!

Each District is run by an Executive Committee who are elected according to the rules by the members and Churches in the area. They have particular responsibilities to the Union and will accept any extra duties that the National Executive asks of them. Ideally they should arrange a reasonable educational and publicity programme within the District for the benefit of the members, and any social activities that they feel will bring the area together as a unit. Most executives also try to arrange regular visits to all the Churches, to try to sort out any problems before they become headaches. One thing that is impressed upon each new member of the Executive Committee is that they are not entitled to interfere with the running of a Church, if that Church is applying the Rules of the Union. Each Church is autonomous and responsible for their own domestic arrangements.

When a medium wants to become certificated, they send a list of their dates to the D.C.Executive, who will then arrange for the required assessments to be done, usually by one of their number, but sometimes using an experienced member of the District. The Executive are then responsible for carrying out a vive-voce, to make sure that the potential certificate-holder has basic knowledge of the Union and their religion before sending a recommendation to the Exponents Committee. This is not the end of the Executives responsibilities; they must re-assess any Certificate or Diploma holders in their District on a regular basis and look into any complaint a Church might make, whether about a worker or about the local council's activities as applied to their existence. When necessary the Executive will report to the National level and ask for their help. They also hold regular general meetings, so that they representatives can make their wishes and requirements known. The District will elect or appoint a representative to be their delegate at National Conference and are responsible for paying their expenses, even as the Churches are responsible for paying the expenses of their representatives.

If you think of the Union as a triangle, then the base line is the level of the District Council. This level is actually the most powerful level, because all belong to that level, although some have work to do on the two other levels.

The National Council

The Council is now the policy-making body of the Union. Each part of the organisation is represented. Each District has their own method of appointment; some elect at their Annual General Meeting and others rule that their elected President is automatically their District Representative to Council. The Class B members have a postal vote; the Lyceum Union and the Guild of Spiritual Healers both appoint their own representative, usually their presidents. The Officers of the Union are also members of the Council and they are the only ones who can be members of both Committees.

At one time the National Council was the ruling body of the Union. The elections were all held by postal vote. The Council was made up of President, Vice-President, three National Councillors elected by the members, and by the churches one Class B representative, who was elected by the Class B members, and there were eight area representatives elected by the churches together with two representatives from the Lyceum Union. The Treasurer was appointed by the National Council.

The National Councillors and the Area Councillors were elected for two year terms and their elections were staggered so that there was a continuity of experience. At that time not every District was individually represented, because the country was also divided into areas. One or two districts might come under one area. The areas were: Midlands, North Western, Southern, Scottish elected one year with London, Northern, South Wales, and Yorkshire elected the next year. Before they moved to Stansted, they used to meet in the Britten Library Room at Tibbs Lane, Manchester, and before that they accepted invitations from any Church or area who would host them.

Membership of the Council tended to be long term, which restricted the choice of people to form the various committees as they were mainly Council. At the A.G.M. in 1964 a motion was passed that 'This meeting noted with approval that the conduct of the affairs of the S.N.U. shall be controlled by two bodies to be known as

(a) The National Council of the Union, which shall be responsible for the policy and general activities in accordance with the Memorandum of Association

(b) The National Executive Committee, which shall co-ordinate, and be responsible for the various functions of the Union, to be effected through various sub-committees... etc.'

As we know, this N.P. was not put into effect until the Three Tier System was introduced in 1975.

The members of the various Districts and Branches instruct their representative to put before the Council any ideas for new, or changes of existing, policy. After it has been properly discussed and voted on they will then pass their reports on to the N.E.C. for any implementation agreed upon. Each member should then report back to those he, or she, represents. This Committee is an important part in the structure of the Union and one which is not always made full use of. Too seldom do the members actually formulate instructions for their representative to take to National level. Each member of the Union can at some point put forward their own ideas. If these are accepted by the majority of their particular group, then they will be put to the group which represents all the members for a general consensus of opinion. Whether the idea is acceptable or not depends first and last upon a democratic vote. Whether they are practicable and of long term feasibility is a different matter, and the N.E.C. will debate this when they are put to their Committee.

The National Executive Committee

The members of this Committee are the Directors of the Company. They are responsible for implementing the ideas that come through the Council and through the motions put at the A.G.M. The President and Vice-President are elected by postal vote every year. They, with the Treasurer who is appointed by the President, are effectively the Managing Directors, the Officers of the Union. The main burden of the running of the Union falls upon their shoulders.The rest are the chairpersons of the Standing Committees. The members must nominate these, but they are appointed by the Officers according to ability. This was one of the main reasons for the change in organisation; the old Council realised that too many Committees were being run by people who were not necessarily the right ones for the job in hand. Each has responsibility for seeing to their own task; the education for all the Courses and literature to go with them, the

95

Exponents for arranging assessments of workers etc. The names of the Committees are self-explanatory; the work involved quite extensive. They must report to the Committee at their meetings and to the members at the A.G.M.

There we have the three tiers of the Union organisation. All composed of members, sometimes interchanging, always trying their best. Succeeding in some directions, failing and learning in others. It is not a perfect system; communications break down and misunderstandings occasionally occur. It is however the system that will take the Union into the next hundred years and as long as it is composed of loyal Union members, then it will continue to improve.

The Trust Company

A Need is met

When National Spiritualism was first organised the main focus of need was to bring societies and churches together under one organisation. This bid for strength in unity and purpose soon developed. As it did so other needs became obvious that had not at first been considered. A number of buildings had, through the efforts of their members, been purchased. In law a building cannot be bought by just any society; it must be done in the name of an individual or individuals. These were the Trustees of the property, holding it on behalf of the members who were paying for the building. Unfortunately unless a Trust was properly completed, the members had no redress if the Trustee suddenly decided to dispose of the building. The members could not claim back their hard-earned money and had to start again from scratch. If the Trustee died, the property was by law considered part of their estate and could be claimed by the heirs. Only goodwill then operated. The heir could do what they wanted. This did not happen too often, but it happened often enough to be seen as a serious problem.

The only way to overcome this was for the main organisation to change its status so that the organisation could hold property. The solicitors investigated and found that there was no easy way for the Federation as it was to do this. The simple solution was for a company to be formed, registered and then be merged with the Federation. This was done and the name and title of 'Federation' was changed to 'The Spiritualist National Union', a company, not for profits, and limited by guarantee.

It took until 1905 for a Model Trust Deed to be drafted. It was in 1894 that J.J.Morse first muted this requirement. No doubt all the furore raised by the need to change status put the subject of the Deed out of people's minds. The members discussed the Deed, were not agreed about the draft presented, and so another was prepared, and circulated to delegates so that it could be discussed at the 1906 Conference. The Trust Deed was finally agreed by members in 1907. Mr. Tallent Bateman, the Union's legal Man, was congratulated in the July issue of the 'Two Worlds' for the'..painstaking way, the calm even delivery, and the penetrating insight he manifested of the requirements of the audience, by means of which he succeeded in piloting through Conference a 'legal dish' which without his presence would have been a standing dish for years'. Mr Parr, proposed that the Deed be accepted, adopted and an order to print be given. Mr. Boddington seconded the proposal and the members agreed wholeheartedly.

The printing and production was not actually completed until 1910. Mr. Hanson Hey, the Secretary, who truly enjoyed the achievements of the organisation triumphantly announced:'We now have the machinery and are empowered to take over the Trusteeship of anything from a temple to a saucepan'. It was not before time. Two buildings had been lost to the movement the year previously, Oldham and Accrington. This should not happen again! Hanson Hey advised members to appoint their trustees in General Meeting, so that they could be removed from position if necessary, or another appointed in their place.

The model was first used in Bradford for Milton Hall, and in 1912 Sowerby Bridge, the first building erected in England for Spiritualism, was handed over to the custodianship of the National Trustees. A list of suitable National Trustees was first published in 1911.

This first Scheme was a Joint Trust Scheme. The Union representatives stood as one half and local Trustees were appointed as well, between two and four of each. There was no expense involved when the National Trustees changed as they represented the Union, which is ongoing. There was considerable expense when local Trustees changed because of the legal formalities. There was room for improvement, but this did not happen until 1940. A Sole Trust Scheme had been talked about for some years and preliminary work had been done. First a certificate was needed from the Chancellor for the Union to act as a Trust Company. When it was granted in 1940 it gave power for the Union to hold property far beyond that granted to most charitable based companies.

The Model Sole Trust Deed was approved by a court and the Chief Inspector of Taxes approved the Deed as creating a Charitable Trust. Now societies could appoint the Union Trustee in perpetuity; they no longer had Trustees but Wardens to represent the Trust Body, i.e.the Union. A similar set-up came into force but the title 'Warden' was used. Wardens or Trustees, the duties of protection were the same. Because a Trustee is ultimately responsible for the debts incurred, the representative must inform the Union if any excessive expenditure is planned in a church or society. For the same reason they must check that proper insurance is maintained and any structural defects reported.

When a Trust Deed is formed the aims of the society are specified. This ensures that the building is used for the purpose for which the founders intended and can not be converted according to the whims of a new membership or committee. The Union can take over existing trusts only if they comply with the essential aims of the Union. Answerable at all times to the Charity Commissioners, the Union must comply with its responsibility and deeds as a Trust Company.

The present conditions of Trusts are under review. Many have been found to be deficient to the needs of the members and the ideals of National Spiritualism. The Spiritualist National Union has always been sensitive to the necessity of revision; it often takes a long time to complete any change because of the many factors involved. But it gets there in the end!

The Fund Of Benevolence

Of course Trusts do not always involve buildings. Quite often they are set up to protect money given for a specific purpose and prevent it being used for any other purpose. The Fund of Benevolence is such a Trust. It was started by Mr. E.W.Wallis, the editor of the 'Two Worlds',in 1894 and Mrs M.H.Wallis, his wife, acted as secretary and administered the Fund until the responsibility was handed over to the S.N.U. in 1901. Although it is now administered by a small committee of S.N.U. members, the Fund benefits all elderly Spiritualists who are in need. Often the help given makes the difference between affording or going without some vital requirement.

The anonymity of the recipients ensures their continued dignity. This has been the case from the beginning. In 1904 their 'modus operandi' was queried and Mrs. Wallis explained that 'No one was identified and every effort was made to save the person in receipt of benefit from feeling pauperised'. She also explained that on receipt of appeal, full enquiries were made, save when a person was well known in the movement. At that time they had just £13 in hand. Among those helped were a young man who needed to recuperate from illness and a veteran who was given a small, but regular, income. Mrs. Wallis stated that 'The fund was not founded as a workers' benefit, but for needy Spiritualists.' Mr. Morse helped quite considerably and there were improvements in donations. The regular Sunday of Benevolence was started and continues to this day; it is the third Sunday in October.

Lilly Shepherd has been the chairperson of the Committee for many years now and does a fine job. As well as helping O.A.P.'s enjoy a week at Stansted, the Fund's contribution means that they do not have to pay the full price. Lilly tries to arrange help when people need to go to a convalescent home after serious illness. Naturally over the years it has become more expensive to give this sort of help. Gone are the years when five shillings was the largest payment made to an individual,and that considered very generous! Fortunately the donations have increased accordingly, although there is never enough for all the demands made upon the Fund. A collection is taken at the A.G.M and many members contribute privately,regularly to this charitable cause, some through a Banker's order, which means that they do not even have to worry about making out the cheque and sending it. Quite a few churches still observe the Benevolence Sunday in October and send all the collection from the Services on that day to the Fund. It is just one of the ways that Spiritualists can help each other

The Spritualist Housing Association

Another is Brandon Lodge at Weston-Super-Mare. This is a home for elderly Spiritualists and is a fine example of what can be done when the different Spiritualist organisations can achieve when they work together. It is only a small home and cannot cope with the elderly sick, but there is need for this place for those who have no-one else to live with and do not want to be alone in their twilight years. The Chairman of the Association, which administers the Trust, is Wilfred Watts. He is helped by a small management committee, all voluntary and representative of the organisations involved.

The London Headquarters Fund

The monies from the sale of Doughty St., the former Headquarters of the old London District Council, were invested in a special Trust. Although the Fund has a particular responsibility to both the London Districts, it finances all their activities, other than social. It also helps the Union to propagate Spiritualism generally.

When the East and West London District Councils agreed to the scheme they had to abide by certain conditions. One was that they should surrender all but a small amount of their accumulated capital to the Fund, the residue to be held in the

Building Fund Pool. They also had to waive their rights to their church and Class B allocation. This allocation is given back to the Districts to help pay for the District expenses. The Fund would now pay for the East and West. This is beneficial to them and to the Union.

The Union is the Custodian Trustee, but the Fund is actually administered by six managing trustees who are appointed. three by the East and three by the West. They are responsible only to the Charity Commissioners and have the responsibility of considering any requests made to them by any District of the Union, or by the National Executive Council on behalf of the Union. Any equipment bought must remain the property of the Fund. Any donations and/ or loans must fall within the guidelines of the Trust as specified by the Charity Commissioners.

The L.H.F. has been a life-saver for the Union in times of extreme financial hardship. For several years they guaranteed an overdraft. This meant a considerable saving on interest charges for the Union. They bought Redwoods, and then only charged the Union a peppercorn rent. They have been responsible for much of the up-dating of equipment for the Head Office. Without the L.H.F. the Headquarters Publishing Company would not have been able to buy the title to the 'Two Worlds', a journal which has always been closely associated with the S.N.U. Finally, many D.C.'s have been able to take advantage of the conditions of Trust; equipment needed for the efficient running of their Districts has been made available.

CHAPTER 13

THE SPIRITUALIST NATIONAL UNION AND THE LAW

To Safeguard our Property

When National Spiritualism was conceived and brought into being by our pioneers it was an ideal, a dream that at last had been realised. At that point it seemed simple to bring so many small groups into cooperation and unity, under one flag. It was not easy; they were all different and individual. The concept of Nationalism in their religion was new. Self-government on such a scale was not part of their previous experience. Gradually, it became obvious that more than a voluntary observance of rules would be needed; a legal status would be required.

The loss of churches and buildings was not great but it was happening. The law was that a building had to be 'owned'. A group of people could not own the building. A group in a position to start buying their church would have to register the sale in the name of an individual. These individuals were called Trustees and in Law they owned the property. Unless precautions were taken, if anything happened to them then the property would pass to their heirs as part of the estate. It could then be disposed of and the members had no chance to regain what was rightfully theirs.

This was not just a financial loss; to the people who had worked so hard to raise the money the loss of heart was even greater. They were not rich; few owned even their own homes. It is one thing to start from scratch, but to lose all through the strength of legality and for no one, even their religious organisation, to be able to help- that was heartbreaking. The need for change was vital and it had to be a legal change for the Federation to be of any use in the matter.

In principle, all agreed. But when advice was taken and it was realised what conditions would have to be met, hundreds disagreed. They learned that under the constitution of the Federation, they were limited. Only by declaring a basis of religious principles could they meet the legal requirements. None wanted to bind themselves to orthodoxy; that was the whole point of the organisation. Members did not want to regress, but to move forward. The Liverpool N.S.C. almost resigned their membership over this vexatious matter. In the end it was agreed to accept the Seven Principles given by Spirit through Emma Hardinge- Britten and first read at Union St., Oldham in 1987as their declaration of belief. The first steps towards legal status were taken and a memorandum stating the aims and objects of the organisation was drawn up. The Principles were adapted as a basis for this. On legal advice, steps were taken to become registered as a charitable company limited by guarantee. Becoming a company meant that we had to have regulations governing the method of running it as a business. These are called 'articles' and specify the relationship between the company and its members or shareholders. Part of this framework are the bye-laws. They ensure the co-ordinated running of the administrative machinery.

Uniformity

Because of the unique character of our religion, many separate groups coming together to form the body rather than one ideal being spread to result in the formation of many churches, it was necessary to instigate Rules so that there would be a solid basis of conformity from place to place, while still leaving each group its autonomous identity. No easy task! It was not until 1902 that the Federation members finally agreed all these details and the transition of title and status was made. The time used for this business at Conference was often resented; keeping it up-to-date is still time consuming. This has always been a bone of contention and remains one of the penalties of democratic organisation.

Over the years, a number of minor changes have been made, some more effective than others. The need to define areas was necessary in order to de-centralise. The formation of District Councils meant changes being made to the Articles and Bye-laws because the Executive Committees of each District undertook to run the affairs of the Union within their own area. Eventually the members of the National Council were representatives of these Districts. Sometimes two Districts would have one representative between them. The Lyceum, even before it became a Branch of the Union, had their representative on the Council which was the ruling body of the organisation.It was not until 1914 that someone realised that each society and branch should have their books audited properly.The churches, societies and individual members within each District are responsible for the election of their own Officers and members of their District Executive. These are often the people who will move on to National committees. In this way everyone has a say, to some extent, in what is going on in the Union.

Many complaints have been, indeed still are, made in reference to the amount of time spent on revising the Articles and Bye-laws of the Union. What is often not recognised is the fact that every time someone puts forward as motion which effectively changes part of the constitution, these have to be checked for reference. If any Article or Bye-law is involved, then nine time out of ten, it will need to be altered to incorporate the members' instructions. We registered as a company with charitable status in order to secure legal standing in Britain. This gave us certain right,s but also many obligations in law. We are answerable not only to the Charity Commissioners, but also to the rulings of the Companies Act. At one time we needed a special Standing Committee just to deal with these points. We have at all times to protect our status; now we have caught up and the Committee has been reduced in size and its status is that of a sub-committee of the National Executive Committee.

The Union used to circulate members, asking them to remember the financial needs of the organisation in their wills. Loyal members responded, but this highlighted some legal difficulties. The Spiritualist medium was not legally recognised and so money left for the development or training of mediums need not be honoured if challenged. The Union actually had two model forms of bequest drawn up to overcome these difficulties and members would be sent these on request. They were subsequently printed in the Union diary.

In the 1930's private streets were still quite common; but many local authorities were taking over and charging individuals for the work done to pave the street properly. Advice was published about the rights of churches in the 'Two Worlds' which continued to allow the Union free pages to circulate its news. The trustee, incumbent or minister could be exempt from the burden of paying for these improvements, but they needed to know how to apply. A certificate of registration for worship was a vital requirement before exemption under the Private Street Works Act could be claimed. One church registered a bare fortnight before notice was served on them by the local Authority, and so saved themselves a considerable amount of money. One church found itself in the unfortunate position of having bought land but not yet being registered, the Trustees had to bear the considerable cost of making up pavement and verge. The Union was able to intervene and help several churches who were affiliated. This was to their benefit as well, because they stood as part Trustee. Many people got a nasty shock when they realised that as Trustee they were personally liable for such bills; if their church could not re- imburse them it was very hard on them and their families. It was matters like these that persuaded the Union to have a Sole Trust Deed drawn up and many churches to adopt this Deed in preference to individuals holding the Trust, together with the Union.

Amalgamation

In 1948 the enormous exercise of amalgamating the B.S.L.U with the S.N.U. took time and effort. It had been decided to leave the constitution of the Lyceum Union as it was, but the constitution of the Union had to be altered in many respects. At first the new branch was known as the 'Lyceum Department'. But a lot of people objected to this and so the name was changed again, back to 'Union' but without the prefix British. They have operated since then as the Spiritualist Lyceum Union. Their accounts are shown in the Union Audit, but form a separate Trust with the Union as Trustee. This was done on legal advice to protect their funds, in much the same way the the monies from the Building Fund Pool are protected against disaster

The second really large change in our history was in 1975. In this year a new scheme, one which had been talked about for some years, was introduced by Gordon Higginson. Prior to that time the Council comprised of about thirty members. The Committees were run by these and the meetings were chaotic, each trying to present their own reports and few decisions being reached. As many had to travel long distances the meetings, which often lasted from Friday through to Monday were very expensive. As it was the Union was financially unviable. The President had travelled the country trying to raise funds just to keep going. He had managed to lend a substantial sum of money from a source which preferred to remain anonymous but this had to be repaid. Every thing must be done to try to make the organisation more efficient. The Three Tier System was introduced to do just that.

It was proposed to have a smaller body who would be Directors of the Company. This would be the National Executive Committee and would be the new ruling body, the people responsible for the actual the running of the Union. There would also be a Council which would be responsible for proposing the future policy. The Council would consist of one representative from each of the Districts and from the two Branches, as well as one person elected by the individual members to represent them. They would take instruction about the policy from their Districts, discuss it and pass on viable ideas to the NEC who would be responsible for putting it into effect. In future, the chairmen of the Standing Committees would not be elected by the members. This system had meant that those who had most support were elected, or those who were willing designated and often this was not the best person for the job. It was proposed that the President, in consultation with the other officers, the Vice-President and Treasurer, would appoint the chairmen according to ability rather than popularity. The members would still have rights; no Chairman could be appointed unless they had been properly nominated by the members. This change in procedure meant quite drastic changes in the Articles and Bye-laws and put tremendous pressure on the Rules and Standing Orders Committee. Somehow they coped. Naturally they had to have a great deal of legal advice. It is quite remarkable how much was managed by people who were not familiar with legal jargon or procedure.

A Medium, A Witch or a Vagrant?

This question has been the most compelling of our history and the fight to remove the stigma of such labels was the longest legal wrangle that we, hopefully, will ever face.

The first mediums to be prosecuted under this ancient Law were Slade, Monck and Lawrence in 1876. In spite of an able defence by the Spiritualist Barrister, C.C Massey, they were convicted under section 4 of the vagrancy Act of 1824. The wording: '..using any subtle craft, means or device by palmis-try or otherwise' condemned mediums, genuine or otherwise, to the threat of prosecution for one hundred and twenty seven long years.

Spiritualists have always been aware that there are charlatans and frauds. The number of times that warnings were printed in Spiritualist literature and journals cannot easily be counted. Some seemingly genuine mediums have been persuaded from time to time to 'confess' to fraud; even the Fox sisters made a confession although they did retract at a later date. The damage done was incalculable. The damage done by those actually caught cheating was worse; and there were many determined to succeed in 'exposing' Spiritualist phenomena.

Efforts had been made to persuade mediums to become certificated. It caused no end of argument both public and private. The Union wanted affiliated churches to use only cer-tificated mediums; some actually agreed to do this. They were accused of bigotry, autocracy and all manner of things. In fact, at this time, the idea was more to try to raise the standard of mediumship on platforms than to protect bona-fide workers. The question of qualification did in time come to play some small part in the fight for freedom, when a national register was compiled. The problem was highlighted in 1910 when a motion was put to Conference decrying the activities of some itinerant groups working in Manchester. These were causing the Manchester District real concern, as they were using the term 'Spiritualist' and were often fraudulent and existed only to make money from psychic phenomena. Legal advice was taken. There was no recourse in law, as the word 'Spiritualist' was not exclusive and could not become subject to copyright. The only action that could be taken was a private prosecution against each individual, where evidence would have to be presented. Apart from the adverse effect this might have on the public there just was not enough money available to undertake such a venture.

The Union, having achieved legal status, was presenting as its cornerstone the proof of survival in communication with the departed; an illegal activity! Its workers were being harried, mediums prosecuted and members sometimes losing their jobs if it became known that they belonged to the Movement. A Freedom Committee was started, determined to work to get the Witchcraft Act repealed and the Vagrancy Act amended. A petition was drawn up asking for a charter which would make provision and give opportunity for the exercise of the psychic faculty under supervision. Further, it asked that..a council should effect the provisions of the charter, the delegates to be chosen from Spiritualist churches. Many disagreed with this Charter because they objected to belonging to an organisation. Some just objected to belonging to a church. Even so they did not see why they should be excluded from being on the council. Thousands of people signed the petition, but it had no effect.

By 1916 the situation was becoming very serious. The War had caused an upsurge of interest in psychic matters. There were so many bereaved. Hundreds jumped on the bandwagon. Mediums set up in back rooms, over public houses, anywhere and everywhere. The police did not confine their attentions to the fraudulent. A Parliamentary Fund was started to support the work being done to introduce a Bill into Parliament. A thousand pounds was raised for this work, and a valuable survey was done by Dr. Ellis Powell LIB.B., D.Sc. (Barrister at law). His report helped to raise funds and support. Sir Arthur Conan

Doyle also helped the fighting committee, but it was to be over thirty years before success was finally achieved.

Sir Arthur Conan Doyle is rightly an Honorary President in Spirit. He not only campaigned throughout the country on behalf of our freedom of religious practice but was the head of a deputation authorised to speak to the government on behalf of the Union in 1930. The manifesto presented was signed by Lady Conan Doyle, Hannen Swaffer, Mrs McKenzie, Mr. McIndoe, Mrs. St. Clair Stobart and Mr. Frank Hawkins. It stated, in part, that 'The claim of the Spiritualist is that mediumship is essential to their religious worship and practice, and the present state of the law discriminates against Spiritualists in a sense which restricts their freedom as compared with all other religions'. It was not until 1951 that the Fraudulent Mediums Act was given Royal Assent and became part of the Law in this country.

CHAPTER 14

THE SPIRITUALIST LYCEUM UNION

Historically

The Lyceum movement is historically linked with the education of children and can take great pride in work and progress that has been accomplished in this field. Although in the early years this was its main function, there is far more done now in the field of adult education.

The Lyceum movement first started in America. After an address by Andrew Jackson Davis in New York, 1863, enthusiastic Spiritualists, having just listened to a detailed account about how Spirit children were taught, immediately set up their own school for the children of Earth.

Andrew Jackson Davis believed that all the different aspects of human nature should be explored. He stated that:'the child is the repository of infinite possibilities, enfolded in the human infant is the beautiful image of an imperishable and perfect being.' He realised that each individual has different capabilities: 'Different minds need different methods' The lyceums were formed into groups so that each member could work at their own level. They were taught to learn verses by rote, to explore the natural world, to breathe properly through calisthenic excercises, to accept responsibility and be prepared to present their work to their fellow Lyceumists.

A healthy mind in a healthy body! Ideas that were not taken up within secular educational systems for many, years.

The concept of Lyceum work was introduced into Britain by James Burns, through the publication of extracts from A.J. Davis's Manual. In June 1866 a Lyceum was started in Nottingham. It was four years before the second Lyceum was started in Keighly and a third at Sowerby Bridge. In the next six years only two others were started. But the idea was taking hold.

When Alfred Kitson became interested in Lyceums he could not possibly have realised that he would become known as the 'Father of the British Lyceum Movement'. To start with, he had little education and had to study hard before he could become the leader of a group, a Conductor. In August 1876 he started his own group which soon moved to Ossett. In 1884 he tried to persuade all the Workers to hold a yearly Conference. Instinctively he recognised the importance of unity and the need to reflect against each other.

1888 was an historic year. Three people made contact and this was to be the impetus that the movement needed for eventual success. Mrs. Emma Hardinge Britten had spent many years working in America. She had taken great interest in the Lyceum movement there and had collected papers and items of information in reference to the work. She had met Mr. Kersey in England and had tried to persuade him to put all this together in a book. Mr. Kersey was reluctant, but had through her influence taken up Lyceum work. Earlier in the year, at the Bradford Conference, Mr. Kitson had advocated the need for a manual to use as a basis for each Lyceum group. No one disagreed but they did not have the money to underwrite the task of publication. Mr. Burns was present and he had proved his support for the Movement. He had been publishing regular articles, written by Mr. Kitson, in his journal, 'The Medium and Daybreak'. Even he could not find the necessary money. In September Mr. Kitson was invited to open the new Lyceum at Newcastle, where he met its first Conductor, Harry Kersey. With these three vital people co-operating, a dummy copy of a manual was produced in time for the Conference in Leeds, 1887. Harry paid for the publication himself, giving the work of printing to a Mr. Billings of Keighly. Naturally, that first edition had faults, but it did not deserve the bitter write-up given by Mr. Burns. He had fully expected to be given the publishing rights and was hurt and that hurt showed! The manual was an immediate success and the following year a Spiritual Songster was produced to complement the verses in the manual. These two publications made all the difference to the progress of the movement; by 1888 there were more than forty societies established and the members were ready for the suggestion of national organisation. In 1889, fifty-seven societies agreed that a draft Constitution should be prepared and this was presented and agreed at Oldham in 1890. The Rawtenstall Lyceum was the first to affiliate.

Within the Constitution provision had been made for an Official Organ and in November that year J.J. Morse started the 'Lyceum Banner'. At first the Lyceum Union gave an annual donation to the paper but eventually Mr Morse gave the paper to the Lyceum Union and Alfred Kitson took over as editor. The 'Banner' is still produced thanks to the untiring efforts of Mrs Doris Davey. She has edited the Banner since 1970 and even helped her father do the printing on a Roneo system during the last World war. Mrs Davey is well known in the London area, having once been the President of the London Lyceum District Council. At Conference in 1901, Mr Kersey announced that he had given the copyright of the Lyceum Manual and the Spiritual Songster to the Union. He also gave the plates used for the printing and so the Union could do its own publishing.

By 1893, thirty-seven societies had affiliated to the Union and Conference agreed that the country should be split into Districts. A year later the new title was adopted, 'The British Spiritualist Lyceum Union'. It was natural with so many people involved in both Spiritual Unions, that the National Union and the Lyceum Union should follow fairly parallel paths. During nearly every Conference of the National Union members were encouraged to support the Lyceums. The children of the Lyceum were given pride of place in the grand procession through Darwen in 1894. A motion put by Mr. Kitson at that Conference,that members should recognise the importance of Lyceum work and should encourage every society to incorporate an affiliated Lyceum, was passed, with great enthusiasm. In 1902, at the last Federation Conference, the Sunday morning address was given by Maggie Oakes, a young Lyceumist. The President, Mr. Johnston, expressed admiration for her ability and stated that not enough support was given to Lyceums. In 1904 the first Lyceum Badge bore the photo of A.J. Davis.

Lyceum work was taking on a number of different aspects. Some of the favourite subjects were social reform, women's emancipation, temperance, local government, the abolishment of child labour and the system of half-time education. The lack of attention some gave to the teachings of Spiritualism gave rise to a rather blunt comment printed in the 'Two Worlds' Magazine in 1909. Hanson Hey, the Secretary of the National Union, deplored the fact that while upwards of a hundred might attend the afternoon Lyceum session, only one of that number could be seen at the Service at night. He concluded that those attending the Lyceum were not interested in the Spiritual but in lighter things! It is true that about that time more interest was being taken in secular education; some Lyceum groups arranged for their members to attend lectures to improve their standards. In the early 1900's many Lyceumists gave up Spiritualism in order to pursue careers in social reform. It is easy to forget how safe we are today,, comparatively, from prejudice. Our religion now is considered fairly respectable although there are still some who will not openly confess to their belief.

From time to time educational systems had been muted for Lyceumists through the 'Banner'. One of the earliest was the introduction of the British Lyceum Correspondence College, a tutorial run by Prof. T Tigon. At B.S.L.U.Conference in 1914 a committee was appointed to compile a syllabus, and in 1915 the three-grade Scheme of education was approved by members and the first examinations held the following May. The Scheme had been developed from a suggestion made by Ernest Vickers in 1910, and was subsequently known as the 'Vickers Scheme'. In 1916 London District started a scheme which developed into five Grades. The 1920 Conference instructed the Education Committee to consider both and they were subsequently amalgamated.

Miss M Kitson and Mr. Connor worked very hard at promoting this within the Union and then helped to link it with a S.N.U. educational system. Also in 1920 Mary Kitson started the Lyceum Guild, again through the columns of the 'Banner'. Its motto was "We live to learn and learn to live." Its aim was to develop the members physically, mentally, spiritually and psychically. They had badges to distinguish what exams had been passed in the Lyceum and were awarded stars to attach to these badges if they had an essay or piece of work published in the 'Banner'. The Guild was an attempt to expand members' awareness outside of the Lyceum and leaned towards a social aspect and is still in existence.

The Lyceum movement, even more so than most National Spiritualists was firmly anti-war. In 1911 a call was published persuading members not to join the Boys' Brigade or the church brigade as these were considered to be breeding grounds for the Army and Navy volunteers. Instead, a Peace Brigade was formed within the Movement. A manifesto was printed on behalf of pacifism; it was signed by Herr Bebel, the German Socialist Leader, and M. Maures, the leader of the French Socialists. The 'Banner' supported and promoted conscientious objection and tried to persuade all members that it was evil to kill even those who attacked. At that time there were over eight thousand members of the Lyceum Union most of whom bought the Banner; Membership actually increased during and just after the first World War, but from the 1920's there was an effective decline. Over the next ten years the number of societies recorded actually increased but while two hundred and fifty-six were admitted to affiliation, two hundred and thirty-eight dropped out.

Co-operation between the BSLU and the SNU increased in the 1930's, particularly in the field of education where joint committees had been formed. A joint education scheme was devised which focussed on the new National Spiritualist College. Students were awarded degrees of Associate, Graduate and Diplomatist, after the successful completion of a three-year course of study and the subsequent examinations. The student had first to complete the five-grade Lyceum Scheme. The College operated until 1938 before being dissolved. The Lyceum Scheme is still in operation, but now attracts very few children. It still gives dispensation within certain parts of the Union Educational system where the two overlap.

Relationship between the two Unions started to deteriorate. By 1937 a resolution was discussed at Conference with a view to severing the ties completely. The situation was not helped by the formation of a National Youth Movement in 1942. The second World War had affected both Unions badly. The Lyceum movement in particular found that the evacuation of thousands of children from the larger towns was disastrous. Those running the Lyceums still existing had to divide their time and found that they were faced with greater priorities. The country was under attack and needed every able-bodied person either for fighting or for defence. Halls were taken over for the War effort and travel seriously restricted. The decline of the Lyceum, started gradually in 1931, increased. After the war the country took quite some time to return to normal. By the time it did, attending a Lyceum was no longer a matter of tradition. Most of the activities were covered in schools; there was no longer the same need, physically or educationally.

From the beginning the Lyceum was a separate body from the S.N.U although it was 'in representative membership with the S.N.U.' Many times suggestion had been made to bring a closer link but these had not been carried through. In 1913 legal advice was taken in order to give the Lyceum Union greater legal powers. One method would be to come into trust, but the advice was against that method at the time. The Lyceum was in 1913 larger and more prosperous and naturally wished to retain independence. The Second World War had disastrous effects on both Unions, but particularly on the Lyceums. The upheavals had forced many to close down and the social climate of the country did not encourage re-establishment in pre-war numbers. By 1946 it made sense to unite.

In 1946 agreement was made to set up a Negotiations Committee consisting of three members from each body. At last, in 1947, it was agreed to unite. Present at this vital meeting were: A.H.Vigurs, John Stewart, Percy Wilson, A.E.Fruin, G.A.Mack, J. Railton and Jessie Greenwood. Jessie had been President of both Unions and had been present at the second annual conference of Lyceums; a year before the Lyceum Union was formed. It was fitting that she should be present at this vital change in formation.The negotiations took time. But finally on May 24th, at Bournmouth, it was agreed by the members that the two Unions should become one organisation, but that there should be a separate department known as the 'Lyceum Department' and that all property, funds etc should be held in Trust by the S.N.U. for the express benefit of the S.L.U.

In January 1948 the B.S.L.U. was incorporated into the S.N.U. as the Lyceum Department. On the 5th June a letter was received from the S.N.U. stating that in future the title would be 'The Spiritualist Lyceum Union'. The unity of purpose would now be strengthened by unity in organisation. As a branch of the S.N.U., the Lyceum would be responsible for the training of the young; the change of name would make no difference to the original intention.

Secular education had caught up with the visions of Andrew Jackson Davis and no one had developed his ideas further. The Central Committee had a tremendous challenge to face. Attendance at Sunday School at one time was automatic; this was no longer the case. The activities which attracted before the war did not have the same fascination to post war youth. They now participated in free expression at school during the week. In 1944 a new six-section scheme was accepted to supplement the old Group System. In 1963 there were special celebrations to commemorate the introduction of the Lyceums one hundred years previously.

In 1977 a joint education committee was set up with the S.N.U. to cover the examinations and other aspects of work. Then in 1983 the Five-Grade System was replaced. The Officers had worked hard to devise a modern equivalent of Andrew Jackson Davis's original vision. The Awareness Scheme is based on 'reward for effort'. Successful completion of the 'Gold' section and a minimum number of Officers' Training modules leads to a Diploma of the S.L.U. The scheme is open to any age group and includes educational and social skills. Music has been introduced to the calisthenics and in some Lyceums this has been replaced with 'keep fit' sessions or 'music to movement'. Modern technology is encouraged, slides, films etc and in some areas rock climbing and canoeing are part of their programme. In spite of all this, the interest of the young is spasmodic and continued effort is constantly required from the officers. Their loyalty and hard work have kept the Lyceum Union alive. The spiritual need remains and it is in this area that the Lyceum will perhaps concentrate future attention. First though, parents must recognise the ability of the Lyceums to add to the quality of their child's life.

There are less than sixty active Lyceums groups in Britain today, most have an adult attendance. Our young parents are the ones who can reverse this trend. The Lyceum has often changed at about the same time as the National Union. There is no doubt that as we move into the second century of existence together, then mutual support and co-operation will be beneficial. We cannot afford to leave the training of our future to chance. Our Lyceum Union remains a vital part of Spiritualism.

CHAPTER 15

THE GUILD OF SPIRITUALIST HEALERS

Healing from the Beginning

Healing has been important in Spiritualism since before the manifestation of phenomena. As Mesmer used magnetised rods to sometimes effectively cure the sick, so it was discovered that some patients went into a trancelike state and were able act as mediums for the production of psychic phenomena. Some mediums found that they had specialised abilities and were able to use these in healing. Andrew Jackson Davis was one such person. He, while in trance state, could see through the skin and flesh to discern the various organs of the body. Without medical training, he was able to diagnose and often to cure ailments that he had never even heard about. After the publicity of the Fox sisters, people became more interested in communication and gradually the focus of attention changed to table-turning. The people of the 19th Century had been raised to largely ignore their ills. The established church tended to foster the belief that suffering was good for the soul, particularly if you were not wealthy or influential! The Lyceum groups in America first recognised that a healthy body helped to promote a healthy mind, and that each child was entitled to grow strong and straight. They encouraged deep breathing and clean living.

The popular interest in healing did not start until well into this century, although there was a Healing Committee of the Council and many individuals practised either at home or, less often, within the societies or Churches. Gradually, as more and more groups came to own their own premises, so this increased. Many people advertised offers of Spirit healing alongside guarantees of 'cures' achieved through either healing or alternate remedies. Much of this was curtailed in 1933 when the medical profession put a Bill to Parliament attacking patent medicines and attempting to make unorthodox methods of healing illegal. A resolution was carried unanimously at Conference that:'this Conference of the SNU protests against the introduction of the Medical and Surgical Appliances Bill, as an attack upon the widespread and long-recognised practice of Spiritual and mental diagnosis and healing and requests every Spiritualist to call upon his Member of Parliament to oppose it in the House of Commons when advised by the National Council'. In spite of this, Ernest Bevin, the Minister for Health, stated that he intended to make the advertising of cures illegal and would attract a fine of up to fifty pounds.. Specific illnesses specified included cancer, cataract, Brights disease and epilepsy. However,it is true to say that although restrictions were placed upon alternative medicine in this country we have a greater freedom than most other countries in the practice of alternative medicine.

Harry Edwards, a very good friend and Minister of the Spiritualist National Union, helped publicise and promote the healing faculty in Britain. He is the best-known healing medium of this century, famous not only in Britain but in many other parts of the world, to bothSpiritualist and non-Spiritualist.

Gradually people requiring healing started to turn to their churches. There they were treated by fellow church members who were attracted to that form of mediumship. At first there were no rules other than common sense and no standard training of the people giving the healing. Because each church is autonomous, it was felt necessary to bring into the rules which govern the organisation certain guidelines. The S.N.U. set up a Healing Committee which dealt with these matters. Now each church is governed in this respect by the Rules as well as the Bye Laws and the Code of Ethics accepted by the Confederation of Healing Organisations; then each individual worked according to his own conviction. When the Union realised that insurance would have to be offered to cover the work being undertaken in affiliated societies, they set about finding the best way of doing this. In 1952 they did indeed offer insurance, although it was not as extensive as is offered today.

The Start of the Guild

Due to the increase of healing within the churches, the Healing Committee put a motion to the 1963 A.G.M. that 'Approved Healers' should be certificated. The following year, at Manchester, a scheme was put forward that a separate entity should be established, called the SNU Guild of Spiritualist Healers. The existing Healing Committee, Tom Henwood, Miss Cliff and Jimmy Biggins among them, would be responsible for organising the new Guild and then setting up Committees in the various Districts. Mr. Tom Ella, the Guild Secretary, shouldered much of the responsibility, together with the existing District Councils, who were asked for their help in this task. It took a lot of hard work. Again, members were suspicious of regimentation. The first Guild Committees were set up in Manchester, South Wales, Southern and the Midlands in 1964, but it was not until ten years later when the North Lancs and Cumbria District had been organised that the whole of the country was covered.

At Stansted, in 1970, on the 10th January, the Inaugural Meeting of the S.N.U.Guild of Spiritualist Healers was held. Mr. Jimmy Biggin chaired the meeting and Mr. Tom Henwood, M.S.N.U. was elected as the first Chairman of the Guild. In July the Guild formally took over the functions of the old Union Healing Committee. Several of the Officials merely changed titles!

Thanks to the work of the Healing Committee the task of the new Guild was made easier. Never-the-less they had a momentous task in front of them. First, they needed members. In 1970 there were only eleven hundred members, but by 1972 the Union recognised that the Guild was developing into a very solid and soundly based organisation. Accordingly, they decided that new bye-laws must be drawn up for its protection and that the Guild should be a Branch of the Union. As a Branch of the Union, the Guild has its own prescribed functions and any duties prescribed from time to time by the S.N.U. The Guild concentrated on individuals rather than on churches and societies. The churches had their own rights to appoint accredited healers.

Any organisation needs funding and collections at meeting do not cover this requirement. The Foundation Fund started in 1979 underwrites the cost of running the Guild. The capital of this is never used, but the interest subsidises any leaflets which do not pay for themselves and the rent of their offices etc. Sometimes special projects are undertaken and in these cases there is money available. Apart from this, the Guild has a yearly subscription fee from its full and associate members to subsidise their activities. In that same year the Union members in Annual General Meeting, agreed that the Guild should have control of its own separate funds, and like the Lyceum Union, their Chairman should be known as 'President' from the 1st January 1980. The Bye-Laws already specified the constitution which was virtually parallel to that of the SNU, the parent Body. Thus in every sense the Guild was a full Branch of the Union.

The Union was obviously still very concerned with the subject of Healing and had an active Education and Exponents Committee(now split into two for efficiency) They instituted an exam in 1978/9 to cover all the aspects of healing, a Course which meant that those interested only in the Healing and not the clairvoyant aspect of Spiritualism would be able to qualify for a Diploma of the Spiritualist National Union as a Healer. This innovation was very popular in theory but the actual Course was not easy. It involved three of the Courses C7, C8 and C9. At first not very many ventured to try these, but soon more and more were encouraged to do so.

Co-operation with the B.M.A.

In 1981 the Guild became with about thirteen other organisations, a Founder Member of the Confederation of Healing Organisations. The idea of the C.H.O. was to combine and then start talk with the Medical profession to convince them that there are definite benefits present in alternative healing which can complement orthodox methods. The ethics adopted by the C.H.O. are taken from the 'Ethics of Healing' originally issued by the S.N.U. and the Guild. The insurance cover has been increased dramatically to come into line with the requirements laid down by the Medical Profession. This was required if the Profession was to agree, even in principal, to work with representatives of the C.H.O. A number of projects were set up to investigate the efficiency of the Healing Forces; the Medical Profession have given limited co-operation to these schemes: but as long as they are agreed in principle, then there is scope for expansion.

From 1980 the Guild has supplied various leaflets and books and tapes on healing and other relevant subjects. These have proved a great advantage, especially where groups are working in outlying areas and do not have constant contact with other groups or their parent Body. Now there are very few churches who do not have their own healing teams working at specified times during the week, often even going out to sick members of their congregation in their homes or in the hospitals. Healing in Spiritualism has never tried to usurp the function of the medical practitioner but rather to complement, to augment the help available

When the simple C17 was introduced it created furore. Members were told that if those training wanted upgrading, they would have to take this Union Course. What was not realised was that it is not an involved Course like the Diploma Course which deals with theory, practice as well as anatomy. From a slow start, this Course very soon became one of the most popular in the Union, possibly because it is now a requirement of Guild membership, but perhaps because more and more people realise the need to have a basis of practical knowledge to complement their spiritual abilities. Focussed mainly on the basic methods, legal requirements and ethical practice of Healing, C17 has been introduced in plenty of time for any possible change in regulations in 1992, when we will possibly come under different regulations due to going fully into the European Community. Those belonging to the Union are of course in a different category than those working outside a religious organisation.

For some years the Guild ran its own week at Stansted. This, although well supported, had to be discontinued in 1988 because there were not enough Guild officials available to organise and to run the week. Instead they have started to hold mini-seminars where one-day work shops are arranged in various Districts. In this way they are able to reach more members who are interested in expanding their understanding of healing capabilities.

From 1963 to the present day the Guild has continued to expand. Plans are in hand to celebrate with the S.N.U. and with the S.L.U. during their Centenary year. Out of the 'Age of Darkness' through the 'Age of Enlightenment' and reaching out for the 'Age of Fulfilment', the Healing Guild will work towards increasing their understanding of the healing process to take their rightful place in modern-day medicine.

CHAPTER 16

SOME NAMES TO REMEMBER

There are many people who should be mentioned in a chapter on personalities of the Union. Some would support a chapter in their own right but this is a small book. A taste of things to come!

Emma Hardinge-Britten was instrumental in calling the first meeting, the forerunner of the Federation which expanded into the Union. Medium, Speaker, editor, missionary, Emma travelled the world propagating the message of Spirit. Thousands listened and learned from her trance addresses. She was the medium to give the basis of the Seven Principles from Spirit and is remembered with respect and pride.

The Union has had some outstanding mediums who have worked for the cause of Spirit. George Berry, former president, writer, diplomatist and lecturer; Helen Duncan, famed for her physical mediumship, 'Battling' Bertha Harris, a minister of the Union who convinced many public figures that survival was a fact. Tom Tyrrell, a brilliant medium who worked in the first half of this century. Horace Leaf, a Fellow of the Royal Geographical Society, lecturer and minister of the Union. Eileen Garrett and Estelle Roberts, prominent in the fight for freedom as was John Stewart one-time president, vice-president and treasurer of the Union who: 'Walked the halls of power in Westminster to persuade M.P.'s to repeal the Witch-craft Act'. Nan McKenzie who worked until she was over ninety years old. Nan attended a Psychic News Dinner Dance in her ninety-ninth year to receive the award of 'Spiritualist of the Year'. She lived to the age of one hundred and one before, 'going home'. Harold Sharpe was one of the first to depict the Aura on paper. Maurice Barbanel, editor of the 'Two Worlds and 'psychic News', valued as medium, supporter and minister of the Union as well as a writer of note he actually passed 'In harness'!. The list is endless; so many more should be mentioned!

One or two of the General Secretaries have made their mark on memory, Hanson G.Hey, a man of conviction, humour, hardwork and staying power. One of his quotations gives an insight into this remarkable man's character: "Man was not made to dwell alone. I believe the welding together of the local forces of Spiritualism would make a national Movement of titanic strength. We need it now because we cannot sit down smug and complacent and say,'All's well in Bradford, it does not matter how the other parts of Great Britain fare!'" George Berry who resigned as president to become the general secretary in 1921. Mr. F. Harris, a natural organiser, systematic and orderly. Qualities needed in the 1930's.

All of our past presidents have achieved some prominence and deserve mention, some for their personalities, all for their work. It is difficult to pick out a few at the expense of the many. Harold Vigurs was a 'legal man' and used his abilities for the benefit of the Movement; he was also a fine speaker, leader, philosopher and a very profound person. Ernest Oaten, one of the many officers of the Union to be associated with the 'Two Worlds'. He was the editor and managed to combine both positions with skill and diplomacy. Known as 'The father of the Council' he joined the Movement in 1893, served on the Council for over twenty-five years and was a very well known trance medium. William 'Sledgehammer' Johnson, with his wealth of white whiskers and beard steered the change from Federation to Union. He was chosen deliberately for this task and fulfilled all expectations. He coupled compassion with a very firm demeanour. This short list must include the only woman to be elected as president of the S.N.U., Jessie Greenwood. A remarkable lady from Hebden Bridge in Yorkshire she was also President of the Lyceum Union as well as her own church. Jessie served on the Council of Hebden Bridge and was the Mayoress there for some time. She came into office at difficult time but being no stranger to problems coped admirably! One person belongs in this list although his name does not appear in the diary as a past-president. Dick Boddington joined the Council before the first World War and became Vice-President in the late 1920's. He stood aside from the Presidency to make way for J.B.McIndoe who had shown his suitability for the post. It was Dick Boddington who secured the rider to the Seven Principles 'Liberty of Interpretation', a clause which has recently been removed upon receipt of legal advice.

We are not without great workers today. Not all have risen to office, not all want to work on national level. The three present officers of the Spiritualist National Union have worked together to steer the Movement through great changes. Their task has not been easy and they have been assisted by a variety of people from all the Tiers of the Union.

Eric Hatton has been the the Vice-President of the Union since 1982. He is a man of strong opinions who always tries to see the other persons point of view. This does not detract from his strength, indeed the resulting balance has emphasised his reasonable attitude to life and living. His speech is quiet but people listen and take note, for what he has to say makes sense. His attitude is modest, he has no false pride! His love of his family has spilled over to many people, always to their benefit.

Eric came into the movement over forty years ago, after the war. He has always been closely associated with the Stourbridge Spiritualist church where he has been president for thirty years. In spite of the extensive travel that Eric undertakes on behalf of the Movement, he is an excellent speaker, an outstanding administrator, he and his wife Heather concentrate most of their energies on behalf of their church. For many years now they have worked together as a 'Healing-team'. Eric has always found time to exercise another gift of Spirit. He has a beautiful singing voice and has won many prizes in competitions. He has a love of operetta,, Gilbert and Sullivan in particular and was once offered the chance to sing professionally with the D'Oyle Carte Company. He refused that offer and went into business where he has been equally successful. Spiritualism is all about balance and exploration of 'Self'. Eric is a balanced man and the Movement is lucky to have him as one of it's foremost advocates.

126

Wilfred Watts is the Treasurer of the Union and has held many different positions within the organisation. He first became interested in Spiritualism as a young man. At the time he was a Sunday School teacher and lay speaker in the Congregational Church. At one of his first visits to a Spiritualist church at Kiverton he was told from platform that he, too, would one day work as a medium. His reply was: 'Not likely'. Fortunately for the Union he was wrong! As a Sanitary Inspector his work took him to many parts of the country. When in Brighton, after the war, he was given a contact from Spirit with whom he had made a pact. He and a friend promised that if either should die and found out that there really was life after death then they would return to haunt the other. John Marsh went first and returned to give his name and informed Wilfred, through the medium that:'He was here to haunt him (Wilfred)'.

He did not become involved in the Union until after the war. He saw an advert in the Psychic News about the educational Courses, responded and has been active since then. When Doughty Street in London opened Wilfred found a niche in which he could develop his many talents. He joined as a Class B member and was soon elected on to the London District Council. He held several positions, Vice-President, Area Representative to Council, Secretary and Treasurer. When Stansted Hall was given to the Union it required a great deal of work and alteration before it could be opened to the general public. Wilfred was involved at the Hall during this period. He was the Bursar for a time and was the first minister to be ordained at the Hall. Mr. Winning Officiated and Longton Choir sang, grouped on the stairs to the Gallery.

In 1965 Wilfred returned to district council work in London. It was not long before the Movement took further advantage of his professional administrative expertise. He sat on consultative Committees mandated to direct the changes of organisation; he was elected on to Council and is, with Gordon Higginson, the longest standing member of the Council today. During his years of office he has worn many hats: Chairman of the Spiritual Housing Association, which administers the affairs of Brandon Lodge, Treasurer of the C.H.O.. Chairman of the Disputes Committee, 'Troubleshooter extraordinaire'. One of his quotations is that:'If you want a dirty job done, choose a Sanitary Inspector to do it.' He is of course part of many other Committees as well as the Council. He has been the Chairman of the London Headquarters Fund since its inception being annually elected to this position.He has continued his interest in education and did a great deal of the work in re-vamping the examination system of the Union. In his sixties he decided that he should undertake yet further studies and, in his spare time, took an Open University degree. He is presently studying the Law. A subject in which he is well versed having worked in the field in various capacities for many years.

Wilfred has combined his national work with the exacting task of President of Croydon National Spiritualist church and the East London District Council. He is also fine speaker and demonstrator. For many years he has chaired Conference. Sometimes known as 'Cavalier Watts' he has a grasp on the affairs of Conference that allow him to make instant decisions which save much wasted time.

CHAPTER 17

GORDON HIGGINSON, M.S.N.U.

That's my Boy!

Mr. Gordon Higginson has been the President of the SNU since 1970, the last twenty years. Born in 1920, son of Fanny Higginson, a well-known and loved medium, he has been a Spiritualist all his life. He is considered to be one of the finest exponent of mediumship this century has known, and now in his seventies he continues in this reputation. He has a delightfully disarming, even cherubic demeanour which masks a man of resolution, dedication and purpose. His is the charisma that Spiritualism needed in its leadership at a time when the Spiritualist National Union could easily have been lost to us, the members, because no one else had the courage to tell us that our help was desperately needed. His foresight, hard work and dedication formed a bridge between possible failure and positive success. He is now the head of a team which reaches down through the different Committees to the very roots of the system, the members.

Born 17th November, 1919, Gordon is a natural medium. He started sitting in his mother's circle at the age of three. At first he had a cushion by her side and used to fall asleep during the seance. By the time he was five he was a member of the Longton Lyceum and had his own chair in his mother's circle. From the beginning he was able to see Spirit and by the time he was ten years old he was permitted to give communication to the members in circle. Gordon had a very close relationship with his mother, but he is the first to admit that she was a very hard task mistress, demanding nothing less than full dedication. He continued to develop under the supervision of Fanny Higginson, and proved to have outstanding potential. His life was very full. He had, as well as his school work, two development circles and piano practice to cope with during the week.

On his twelfth birthday, Fanny gave him a most unusual present, one she stated he:'"Would remember all his life." He was allowed to take his first service at Longton Spiritualist Church. This was a great trust. Fanny had been a member of and worked in Longton Church since she was a girl of eighteen. Many people have heard Gordon tell the story of how pleased he was that the meeting had gone well, until he met up with mother. She had listened from downstairs, was not amused and ordered him back to circle. I feel sure that that statement hid great mother's pride. Fanny knew that her son had great potential and probably had no intention of exposing that potential too early in his life. She was a great medium herself, wise and kind, if a trifle direct in her manner. She has been passed to Spirit now for over ten years, and still people send flowers for her birthday and passing anniversary to the church in remembrance. Under her direction Gordon continued his development. As soon as he qualified, age-wise, he automatically became a member of Longton Church.

Although Fanny had said 'back to circle', and meant it, she had started to take Gordon around to share her Services. Soon he was being booked in his own right and she went to support and supervise. She arranged for him to work with other mediums and gradually his circle of experience widened. By the time he was sixteen, Gordon had worked in some of the largest halls in the country. He was never a professional medium. On leaving school at fourteen he continued his education and went to Wolverhampton Technical College studying advertising, window dressing and publicity. These subjects were of use to him when he started work. He went into the shoe trade, buying for a large company and eventually becoming a Director of that Company. It is interesting that his grandfather and great grandfather were both master shoe makers. His father was equally artistic; he was a maker of specialised teapots.

They're in the Army Now!

The war interrupted many peoples lives, creating a vacuum. Not so with Gordon. He considers this time very valuable in that he found out a great deal about himself. Up to then he had concentrated mainly on his spiritual progress and had not had much time to get to know people outside of Spiritualism Even in the army he soon became known as a medium. Every soldier had to wear an identity disk bearing their name, rank, number and religion. The hierarchy refused to put 'Spiritualist' on his disk. They offered a choice, Methodist, Baptist, even Wesleyan. Faced with his refusal to wear the disk they called him to task. They offered an explanation, the word was too long; a compromise: 'Spiritism', Gordon held out and eventually won the day. He later found out that another famous medium, William Redmond, had fought the same battle and had also won through.

There are many psychic experiences that could be recounted about Gordon's sojourn in the forces, but the most interesting is that of when he was in Italy. The company advanced across a river over a virtually un-usable bridge. They met with unexpectedly heavy German troops and were unable to retreat. The bridge had by now collapsed and the river was very fast flowing. They took shelter in a farmhouse. They soon becoming surrounded by tiger tanks, and facing capture or death the instructions were to fight to the last man The Commander approached Gordon. "Do you feel that you are going to die tonight?", he asked. "No" was the swift reply. "Do you want to risk trying to lead any men willing to follow you across the river?" "Yes" came the equally swift reply. Approaching that torrent, fed by the winter rains, even Gordon was a little worried, but he summoned all his courage, stopped and asked his life-long companion from the Spirit world for help. Named 'Cuckoo' because of the games of hide and seek played in his childhood, his guide, a young girl, showed him a ball. "Follow it!" she said, and weaving backwards, forwards and even sideways Gordon did. His men, wondering perhaps if they were being led astray, also followed. Having reached the far, comparatively safe shore they asked Gordon why he had deviated. 'Oh', said he, 'I was following a ball'. They were safe but confused, until they remembered Gordon's reputation as a medium. If Gordon Higginson said he was not due to die that day then the safest place to be was at his side! There is a man living in Longton today, not a Spiritualist and married to a Jehovah's Witness, who won't let her speak one word against Spiritualism. He was one of those who followed Gordon across the river that day. It is sure that those beside him as they were evacuated from the beaches of Dunkirk were equally relieved to have him close by.

A Life's Work

After the war Gordon resumed his life's work. The war had given him experience of meeting and mingling closely with people who had no knowledge of Spiritualism, men from all different backgrounds both personal and religious. Deep within, Gordon recognised the need for all men to come together in unity. Perhaps he had always known this, but needed the sometimes bitter and tragic experiences of conflict to come to terms with instinct. He was not yet ready to work directly to achieve this end; his work did not yet lie in organisation. He was a member of the Spiritualist National Union. Through his membership of Longton he had been since he was eighteen. At present he had to fulfil his destiny as one of the greatest mediums we have known, and that meant work and more work.

His first London Service was at Croydon, Bedford Park; before long he had worked at the Marylebone Association, the Victoria Hall; he was booked for five years running to take the London May Convention. He has worked with the greatest mediums and in the largest halls. Indeed, apart from William Redmond, M.S.N.U., who still works occasionally, he is the only one left who has done. When asked, he recalls names like Harold Vigurs, Shaw Desmond, Nan Mackenzie, the list is endless, shortened only by time and space. He has always worked to capacity crowds, even at the Royal Albert Hall which hold some five thousand people where he sometimes took a Remembrance day Service with people like Magdalene Kelly from Scotland,

Coral Polge of the S.A.G.B., Doris Collins, (now retired and moved to Milton Keynes). During these years Gordon was not only demonstrating but teaching. He took regular lectures at the S.A.G.B., Belgrave Square and many other venues as well as his own church and, of course, at Stansted Hall.

From the age of about twenty-nine, Gordon started to sit to develop his faculty as a physical medium. The circle met in the upper room of the church every week. Even when someone was away for holidays or such, they sat down at the right time to mentally link in with the circle. In this way a continuous appointment was kept with Spirit and the results of that circle reflect the dedication of the members. We will not specify all the phenomena;suffice it to say that at one time there was so much energy available that a spirit form walked nearly the length of the church, shook members by the hand and was as solid to them as you are to each other. For twenty-five years Gordon kept faith with his circle, as they with him. It was only poor health in the end which forced him to close the circle. Many mediums, particularly physical mediums, are susceptible to diabetes. Gordon was told to curtail the amount of sugar in his diet. So much energy is used during a seance of this nature, he could no longer afford to sit on a weekly basis. However the solid work of development had been done and up to now Gordon has demonstrated physical mediumship to more people than any other recorded medium. There were three hundred present to watch full materialisation at the Glasgow Association, and there have never been less than ninety at his public demonstrations at Stansted. It is not easy to arrange these sessions; there are so many dangers in allowing virtual strangers to be present during the manifestation of physical phenomena. Gordon has been injured several times. Burns and bruises were caused through silly actions taken by people who do not realise the amount and quality of energy being used, or the danger to the medium, who is the focal point of that energy. Over the past few years Charles Sherrat, the Manager of Stansted, has had the momentous task of ensuring that Gordon is made as safe as humanly possible from sudden interruption, noise and light. Not easy with over ninety eager, and occasionally ignorant, guests in attendance!

Temptation!

Gordon has expressed some concern that this aspect of his mediumship has not been the best part of his work. Other duties and his health have prevented him from developing his faculty to its full extent. He states that although he has demonstrated to larger audiences than anyone else known, he admits that the phenomena at smaller seances were often better. The greater quality was sometimes sacrificed so that many more people could witness the wonder of physical mediumship for themselves. He has never demonstrated physical phenomena for profit. He has been offered as much as £1,000 for a single private sitting and has refused the money. This is not because he does not appreciate the need for money in life, but because he felt he might be tempted to work for the wrong motive. He stated, with delightful candour: "I was nervous that I might find it too easy to earn money like that. I like nice clothes and a nice house. Once I allowed myself to be tempted I might go on giving in to temptation and that wouldn't have been right." He went on to say that his demonstrations are curtailed now. He is doing less and less physical work because age and health conditions are dictating that it should be so. This is a sad loss to Spiritualism, and the Spiritualist who can often only read about the great seances of the past. Thanks to Gordon's public work in this field, there are thousands who can look back and remember that they did have the opportunity, however briefly!

Gordon Higginson became well-known and well-loved. His main work was as a clairvoyant, speaker and teacher. He travelled the length and breadth of Britain taking meetings and seminars. Fortunately he had moved into business for himself and so could afford the time. Still 'in shoes', he had built up a supermarket, sold at a profit and then started again. In this way he could put in managers to run his business from day-to-day and still have the money to subsidise his mediumship, for few make profit from churches. Mediumship has never been his living. He has put his trust in the churches and in the Union, and although he has been hurt many times by others, that trust remains and is strong. It was inevitable that he would be moved towards office within the Union, even though he was not personally drawn towards the administrational side of our religion. Having attended General Meetings, he realised that the Union was going through a very bad period and responded to repeated requests to stand for National Executive Council, the system that preceded the National Executive Committee. In 1964 he was elected by the Class B members to become their representative. By 1969 he had risen to the position of Vice-President and in 1970 he was properly nominated and subsequently invited to accept the position as President. There was no way that Gordon wanted the weight of that responsibility. For a number of years the administration had become more and more confusing; the financial position of the Union was dire. Liquidation could not be long postponed. But Spirit had other plans in mind!

Man Proposes, Spirit Decide Otherwise!

Gordon had been working at Portsmouth Temple. Returning home in the early hours he took a wrong turning and realised that he was heading for Stansted Hall. He stopped, phoned Mr. Sills, the Manager, explained what had happened and begged a bed for the night, as he was falling asleep at the wheel. Although the hall was closed for the winter months, Mr Sills agreed to get a bed ready and told Gordon that he would be alone but was welcome. Arriving about 3 o'clock in the morning, Gordon ate the sandwich prepared for him and went at once to bed. In the morning when he went down for his breakfast Mr. Sills told him that there was a man waiting to see him. 'That can't be right,' said Gordon, 'no one knows that I am here. I should be at home, not here at all! I think that you had better tell him that I can't see him.' Mr. Sills persuaded Gordon to meet the person briefly and said that he was in the library waiting. Gordon went into the library, saw a monk standing there and went back out after excusing himself. He found the manager and told him that there must be a mistake, that he did not know any monk. "That is who asked to see you," said Mr. Sills. Gordon went back to the library to be told by the monk that he should have expected the visit. His actions had been influenced by Spirit, so that he had ended up at Stansted the previous night and he, the monk, had a message for Gordon. The message was that Gordon had great work to do and that it was important that he did not refuse the position offered to him. Gordon argued he did not want the Presidency. The monk stated firmly,'you must take it, you are needed!' Eventually Gordon left the library to tell Mr. Sills what had occurred. They stood in the gallery, within sight of the library door, speaking about the incident and then both returned to the library, to speak to the monk together only to find that there was nobody there. The monk had gone; how they could not fathom. There is only one door to the library and that had been in full view of them both. Mr. Sills was in no doubt: "You must do as you have been told, you must phone Dick Elleridge and accept the nomination". Gordon did. He became the President of the SNU and remains so today. Apart from the Treasurer of the Union, Mr. Wilfred Watts, B.A.,M.S.N.U., he is the longest serving member of the Council, which is now the NEC. His service at National level had been twenty-six consecutive years,unrivalled by any other person in the Union.

At the Conference that first year he stood up and told the members how serious the position was and promised that if he could not improve the situation within three years he would stand down. At one point the Union owed over forty thousand pounds to the bank. No cheques would be honoured; no cheques could be issued. Gordon started a campaign to raise funds. He travelled the country taking services and begging for donations. Maurice Barbanel and Harry Edwards were a tremendous help in this campaign. They both assisted, and even gave money to save the Union financially. Within three years the greater part of the debt had been repaid, although they were not yet in the clear. Many people rallied to the cause not all of them well known. No other President had spoken out and explained what the true position was. When Gordon did, then the churches and the members realised that they were needed. They responded; we survived!

Gordon had realised very early in his career that Spirit intended to use, indeed had probably inspired, Spiritualism to bring about a unity of nations. He sees Britain's entry into Europe as an extension of that purpose. He states: "The Christian cannot bring the Jew into a religious unity, the Moslem cannot bring the Buddhist. Spiritualism, by standing apart from all these religions,can bring all men together. This is vital for the future, and that is why it is so important to preserve National Spiritualism as it is. We are not a part of any other religion. Spiritualism stands alone as a religion in its own right." He felt right from the beginning that Stansted was important in this scheme, together with the Union. This is why, although Stansted was for many years the greatest drain on the financial resources of the Union, he has stood firm on his promises that it would remain and would not be sold. He is the Principal of the College and was instigator of moving the head offices of the Union from Manchester to the Annexe at Stansted. There are very few weeks when he does not work there at least one day, not only to add to the lustre of the programme but to share the vast knowledge and experience contained in his memory.

Before Gordon became the President, he had muted the change in the administration of the Union. He sat on the Committee and eventually engineered the change from the old Council to the Three Tier System, which is operating today and which is more efficient. He has changed the essence of the Office of President, making sure that he is in constant touch with the members. Many he knows by name; his memory for that sort of detail is phenomenal, even though it can fall short in other directions! His love, compassion and sincerity cannot be doubted. Under the Presidency of Mr. Higginson the Union has moved into a better financial position. We still do not have the resources to be able to relax; there are times when we have to accept loans to 'see us through'. The propaganda work inspired by his example and undertaken mainly by him during this Centenary year should help yet again. Organisations can seem too big sometimes; the

137

charismatic presence of Gordon Higginson through this past twenty years has moulded ours into a pattern. It is big, and we hope will get bigger. We have an example of how one man can change the face of a religion without altering its direction by Spirit, or compromising the democracy of the people. With that example to follow how can we fail to grow?

CHAPTER 18

ONE HUNDRED - AND NOT OUT

Through the Years

From just a few churches and few members the S.N.U. has grown to be one of the largest National Spiritualist organisations in the world. The education programme has expanded and now covers all aspects of theoretical Spiritualism; the practical side, being of equal importance, is also catered for. All the Diplomas cover both areas and are assessed at National level, as is the Certificate of Recognition. This has helped to standardise the levels of ability needed to qualify for a 'pass' and has minimised the possibility of accusations of favouritism which have occurred in the past.

Over the years the complexities of running the organisation have grown proportionately. More paid staff are desperately needed, but the state of the Union's finances have so far precluded this possibility, although an assistant General Secretary is 'in the offing'. The help of the London Headquarters Fund in supplying up-to-date computer systems is having a marked effect on efficiency; the loyalty and hard work of the office staff cannot be questioned and is much appreciated.

In spite of all the despondent remarks made about standards of mediums, this has probably improved. Members expectations are more sophisticated; never-the-less, the standards are still not nearly high enough and plans are in hand for further training programmes. As it is, there are many, many more applying for Certification and literally thousands participating in the various Education Courses of the Union.

The work of Spirit communication has obviously changed over the years. More mediums work on the mental level now rather than the physical. Many regret this change but it has opened the field of possibility to many people who do not have the faculties of physical mediumship. The days of the really great 'Speakers' has died a death! It is hoped that this can be revived but,not in the same way because social conditions have changed. Large halls could be filled quite easily, not just because of the quality of the Speaker, but because there was little else in the way of entertainment. These days people are conditioned to having what they want put in front of them and have to be persuaded to make an effort. Few will travel long distances unless something really special is presented.

The standard of Spiritual literature produced has also changed. The solid books on philosophy, apart from a few exceptions, were written years ago. The trend has shifted to autobiographies. Mediums record their life-story, but seldom the wisdom of their Spirit helpers! Whereas not everyone is agreed on what is wisdom, a choice of different philosophies can help the individual reader to reflect upon what is right for them and to expand their own ideas.

What of the Future?

What indeed! A wave of idealism had been re-awakened. Members are making it known that many want more emphasis on teaching and philosophy and less upon communication for messages. Most want to expand their personal awareness to some degree. A different, deeper way is needed for the next one hundred years. The pioneers had dreamed of a way, a philosophy, a religion which could change the face of the Earth. God knows, as the world approaches the twenty-first century, it is obvious that such a way is needed.

People generally are recognising the lack of balance which endangers the species of Man; the world is turning to a concern about the ecology. During the last decades more and more young people are accepting a personal responsibility for themselves and for their surroundings. Some have greater success than others, but the search is a manifestation of the internal recognition of need. In the fifties they turned to each other, seeking an answer in 'free love' and wild music. In the sixties they turned to 'peace'; the flower people opted out of life as it was. The seventies were far more violent as their rebellion erupted into gang warfare and the use of hard drugs. This vied with esoteric meditations and Spiritual exploration, taking us into the eighties. The dangers of the Atom Bomb were even more highlighted, and those who objected to the misuse of the environment showed their feelings by clashing with those in authority. Animals were let loose, stores selling furs set on fire, tanks physically prevented from moving. Extreme measures reflecting an urgent, if instinctive need for action.

Gradually though the pendulum has ceased its extreme oscillations. Still the need is obvious. More interest is being taken in alternative medicines. The oppressed are being freed and the store of dangerous weapons diminished. People are willing to pay more for recycled goods and for those which will do the least harm to the earth: At last, the Age of Aquarius is beginning to take effect.

What then of us? What are we as a Movement offering to this new and exciting age? Where are we going?

Up to now we have spent time and effort to justify Spiritualism, to forge the organisation into an ongoing movement which can survive for another hundred years. In doing so we have allowed our sights to become dimmed to the reality behind our cornerstone. It is no good chanting 'There is no death' if we cannot move beyond that knowledge. Each one who lives will face physical death and will find out that death is an illusion. No matter how a person lives on earth, they too will survive! That is the Law, not chance and not faith.

In spite of the many who are truly thinking about life and living, making effort to improve not only the quality of their own existence but also that of their brother's life, there are many, many more who do not think this way and see no reason for doing so. Some leaders of nations are making determined effort to restore freedom to their people; others prevent even the hope of this. We have a long way to go!

As Spiritualists our ways must change to keep pace with the future; we, as a Union, have changed quite radically as an organisation. Is that all we are destined to be? Spirit took a long time introducing this religious philosophy on to the earth. It is surely not co-incidental that we are even now celebrating one hundred years, a century of effort, tears, success, and failure. In that time we have become legally recognised and generally accepted. Not how-ever as perhaps Spirit originally intended. Who, but for a few committed Spiritualists, visualise a world-wide religion of Spiritualism? All men joining together under one banner of effort and intent! It was for this very possibility that the Union, as a Body, has resisted all efforts to incorporate a bias towards Christianity. They had nothing literally against the Christian ideals except their parochialism; that limits religion to the 'chosen', the 'believers'. The same resistance would have been meted out to Islam or any other traditional and parochial religion. We cannot limit our possibilities.

There will always be a number of people interested in the phenomena of Spiritualism. Many of these will not require more, just yet! Churches did not decry the philosophy which gives depth and meaning to 'proof' that Man survives the trauma called death, but this was not the part of Spiritualism which generally attracted members. Over the years many have taken the easy pathway and gradually offered more and more of what was wanted, rather than what was needed. It is easy to look back and judge, not so easy to see the church doors close for want of funds. Committees faced with this possibility expanded the side of Communication, which attracted members and minimised the Teachings which attracted the few.

The time for offering just proof of survival is past. The age of individual, great mediums is passing! All people are part of the Great Spirit; all people 'have the capacity of infinite possibilities!' Many will and have discovered this for themselves, and are exercising their minds to make a closer link with the eternal part of Self. There are many more who will need help. We can offer that help! They will not discover this capacity through a reliance on other people who are able to contact and communicate with Spirit. This will probably always be part of the Spiritualist activit,y but will be expanded to be used in a different way. We need more than a constant emphasis upon 'proof of survival' given by mediums who work according to their capacity.

We will not achieve this overnight. Even now there are plans to give further training to those capable of training others. We are expanding our education programme gradually, so that all people who want will have access to knowledge. We will train some to work at the larger publicity meetings, not just as demonstrators, but as speakers capable of conveying the possibilities that Spiritualism offers to all. We are making determined effort to put the Union into a solid financially secure position, for all these plans will take money.

Perhaps by the time we celebrate our bi-centenary every person present will be able to make a good link with their own Higher- Self, and some link with other Spirit, discarnate. They will come together in the same unity that we have this year, from even more diverse and varied backgrounds. Perhaps by then Spiritualism will have become so universal that it will no longer need a label of identification! Perhaps, perhaps..

In first things unity,
In details liberty,
In all things charity.

E.A.Keeling, President of the Spiritualist National Union
1929

THE PRINCIPLES OF SPIRITUALISM

1. The Fatherhood of God.

2. The Brotherhood of Man.

3. The Communion of Spirits and the Ministry of Angels.

4. The Continuous Existence of the Human Soul.

5. Personal Responsibility.

6. Compensation and Retribution hereafter, for all good or evil done on earth.

7. Eternal Progress open to every Human Soul